Say What?

Say What?

A Biblical and Historical Journey on the
Connection between the Holy Spirit,
Prophecy, and Tongues

Jeremiah Campbell

Foreword by Joseph Castleberry

WIPF *&* STOCK · Eugene, Oregon

SAY WHAT?
A Biblical and Historical Journey on the Connection between the Holy
Spirit, Prophecy, and Tongues

Wipf & Stock
An Imprint of Wipf and Stock Publishers
199 W. 8th Ave., Suite 3
Eugene, OR 97401

www.wipfandstock.com

PAPERBACK ISBN: 978-15326-4699-7
HARDCOVER ISBN: 978-1-5326-4700-0
EBOOK ISBN: 978-1-5326-4701-7

Manufactured in the U.S.A.

To John Campbell,

an amazing dad
who taught me
what it means
to be a man of God.

Contents

Contents

Foreword

THE PENTECOSTAL MOVEMENT THAT swept the world in the 20th Century changed the face of world Christianity forever. In short, its unashamed emphasis on the immanent power of the Holy Spirit and its unabashed testimony of Christ with signs following has led to the greatest period of expansion the Christian faith has ever seen. As a result, theologians from every corner of the church had to return to the Scriptures to see if Pentecostal teaching held true. They may not have accepted the central Pentecostal distinctive that speaking in tongues constituted the initial physical evidence of the Baptism in the Holy Spirit, but on the whole, they concluded, overwhelmingly, that miracles did not cease at the end of the apostolic age and that the Bible teaches a larger role for the Holy Spirit than they had thought. I have talked to leading theologians across denominations, and an increasing number of them grew up in Pentecostal homes or spent years in a Pentecostal of Charismatic church. Large numbers of them privately speak in tongues. Virtually all agree that they Holy Spirit still works miracles in response to the bold faith of believers. More importantly, Pentecostalism has affected the spirituality of churches across the worldwide Christian community, as a trained eye can easily observe in a random visit to almost any worship service.

Why has Pentecostalism experienced such stunning success around the world? The success does not flow from placing the Holy Spirit at the center of our theology or even our practice. Rather, it springs from the fact that our doctrine of the Spirit puts Christ at the center. The four-fold Pentecostal Christology declares that Jesus saves, heals, endues with power, and will soon come again. In saving us, Jesus works through the Holy Spirit, who convicts us of our sin and participates in our new birth. In healing us, Jesus ministers the healing power of God to our bodies through the Spirit. Jesus endues us with power by baptizing us in the Spirit, giving us access to the same power that he depended on in his life of miraculous ministry and in his resurrection from the dead. When Jesus comes again, he will raise the living and the dead by the same Spirit that raised him, and he will pour out the Holy Spirit in judgment over evil. Pentecostals do not emphasize the Holy Spirit to lower Jesus from his place of pre-eminence, but rather to exalt him to the front and center of the Christian life.

The theological contribution of Pentecostals over the past century offers a great blessing to the church. This book offers an outstanding summary of Pentecostal thinking about the Holy Spirit, beginning with its reading of the Bible's teaching. It continues to read the history of the Church in terms of Pentecostal perspectives on the Spirit. Whether readers encounter this text as seminary students, as serious, thirsty believers, or as fully-formed professional theologians, they will find a valuable trove of information and wisdom. I pray for every reader that this text will drive them into the presence of God, where the Holy Spirit will make Christ known to them more than ever before.

Joseph Castleberry, Ed.D.
President, Northwest University
Kirkland, Washington

Introduction

A Boy and a Life-Changing Moment

My Story

I REMEMBER THE FIRST time I almost cut off my finger. As a little boy, my dad's hunting knife always seemed so big. He taught me that knives are tools and we should always keep them very sharp, like a razor. If he really wanted to, my dad could shave his face with his hunting knife. One of my most clear childhood memories happened with that very same knife. My dad took me camping, and as an eight-year-old boy, I was in heaven. He taught me how to properly use a knife while I carved a piece of wood by the fire. As I struggled to whittle, I switched the blade and angled it toward my hand. It slipped and I sliced my knuckle. To this day, decades later, I still have the scar.

It's amazing how things stay with you for life, like a scar. I love camping and the outdoors. Growing up in church, we had a program that focused on just that—Royal Rangers. The program reflected the traditional Boy Scouts, but with a spiritual emphasis too. My dad happened to command our outpost, and I remember another time he took me camping, just as vivid in my mind. This time though, more than a thousand other boys had joined us. We had competitions shooting, archery, throwing tomahawks, canoeing, tying knots, making fires, first aide, and all kinds of other survival skills. I loved it.

Each night at the camp we would also have a church service. One night, as a nine-year-old boy, I remember worshiping and seeking God with all of my heart. As I prayed, something other than English began to flow from my lips. I remember the same fear and surprise as the day I almost lost my finger. I experienced such a new sensation and didn't quite know how to process it. Fortunately, that night my dad had accompanied me. He smiled and began to teach me about what the Bible says about the gift of speaking in tongues.

As I grew older, I became aware that very different views exist about the gift of tongues and its role in the Church today. Over the years, different people told me that I had to speak in tongues to be saved, others told me that tongues ceased when the people in the New Testament died and I was demon-possessed if I spoke in tongues. I really didn't know what to make of this gift and had more questions than answers. As I asked people what they thought, I found that most of them just regurgitated what they learned. Others only spoke from their experience, or lack thereof, and still others gave biblical support but often out of context.

Therefore, from my teenage years, I began to search the Scriptures and read all that I could on this subject. I didn't just want to believe something because someone else taught me, or because I had, or hadn't experienced it. I wanted to believe it because of what the Word of God showed me. Consequently, this book has been in the works for more than two decades, as it is a result of my own journey. By no means do I pretend to know all the answers. However, I give a panoramic perspective of this controversial experience of the baptism in the Holy Spirit and its connection with prophecy and tongues throughout the Bible and today. I hope and pray that it gives you something to consider with your own walk with God and what his Word says on the matter.

Part I

Understanding the Role of the Holy Spirit within the Trinity

BEFORE WE GET INTO the nitty gritty of this book, and the work of the Holy Spirit, we need take some time to understand him, and his role within the Trinity. Many misunderstandings exist about the Holy Spirit, and some people just plain lack knowledge about him. So we'll start with the basics here. This first part of the book by no means develops a comprehensive pneumatological study (a fancy way to say "study of the Holy Spirit"), but it does give us a good foundation to understand the rest of the book.

Chapter 1

Who Is the Holy Spirit?

The Trinity

FOR SOME PEOPLE, WHEN they talk about the God of the Bible, they think about the Father and the term Yahweh, or Jesus Christ. Few people think about the Holy Spirit. So, to understand him we need to begin with an understanding of the Trinity.

Many people easily think about God as the Father, and about Jesus the Son because he came in human form. However, they struggle to think about the Holy Spirit as a person. We have to realize that God exists far beyond our understanding. Therefore, as simple humans, we relate the different persons of the God-head to things that we can comprehend. A father is something tangible, and Jesus Christ walked with humanity; therefore, we can grasp him. However, for many people, they understand the Holy Spirit like the force in Star Wars—as an energy or power, and that is where they go wrong.

The word "what" would incorrectly describe the Holy Spirit, rather we must use the word "who" when referring to him. God is one and exists in three persons as Father, Son, and Holy Spirit. The Holy Spirit is not a divine influence, not a cloud, not a phantom, nor a concept. He is a person who possesses an intelligence, a will, and emotions. He is God—with all of the attributes of the deity. The Holy Spirit exists as the third person of the Trinity—on par with God the Father and God the Son—this tri-unity does not constitute three gods, but rather one God manifested in three persons.

People try to define the Trinity, but God exists beyond our understanding. However, a couple of popular illustrations help us understand him to a degree.

Some say that the Trinity resembles an egg. Like the Trinity, the egg has three parts, the shell, the white, and the yolk. Though the egg has three parts, it is still one egg. Yet the egg metaphor falls short because God does not exist in three parts, all three persons of the God-head are one God, none exist as just part of God.

Some say that the Trinity resembles a hot cherry pie right out of the oven and cut it into three equal pieces. You see three equal parts in the crust, but when the knife passes through the cherry filling, it flows back together remaining as one pie on the inside. This metaphor is great, and delicious, but also limited, because it doesn't quite capture the complexity of the Trinity. So, let's take a look at a biblical understanding of the Trinity.

Some have difficulty with the fact that the word "Trinity" doesn't appear in the Bible. However, the lack of the word does not mean that the concept of the Trinity does not exist in the Bible. If we take a deeper look at the linguistic context of the Bible, we will see that the people of both the Old Testament, and the New Testament saw the Father, the Son, and the Holy Spirit as one, and the same God. So let's not just look at what the Bible says about God, but how it refers to him also.

The Old Testament

In the Old Testament, God revealed his name, Yahweh or Jehovah, to Moses at the burning bush in Exodus 3:14, stating that he is "I AM". This Hebrew word essentially means "existence", which appropriately describes God since without him, nothing exists.

The Hebrew people revered the name Yahweh/Jehovah to such a degree that they prohibited its verbal utterance. Their reverence for God's name reflected the third commandment, "You shall not misuse the name of the Lord your God, for the Lord will not hold anyone guiltless who misuses his name" (Exodus 20:7). The Hebrew language does not use vowels; therefore, pronunciation of written words seemed to vary. So, the pronunciation of God's name varies as well—Yahweh or Jehovah.

Interestingly I learned that scribes also revered God's name in writing. Some years ago, the Dead Sea Scrolls exhibit toured Seattle, near where I lived. Although I can't read ancient Hebrew, seeing the fragments in the exhibit fascinated me. As I stared at the writings, I noticed that the same word seemed to stand out in various places, as if the writer had put it in bold for some reason. I pointed out the word to one of the exhibit scholars and asked him what it stood for. He smiled and explained the use of the word Yahweh, the name of God. He went on to tell me that the ancient Hebrew scribes held the name in such esteem that when they copied texts and came to God's holy name, they would lower their pen, pick up a separate pen and use a special ink dedicated exclusively to writing his name. As a result, God's name also stood out in all of the documents as something special, something set apart, something holy. The biblical authors also used this most holy name, Yahweh or Jehovah, to refer to all three persons of the Trinity, (Father, Son, and Holy Spirit) (Martin, Brook and Duncan, 1992, 112).

Moses provides a great example of the special use of the term Yahweh/Jehovah with the Israelites in the book of Deuteronomy. This generation grew up during the forty years in the desert and knew little of what God had done in the generations before. Moses took the opportunity to write about the Father stating, "Hear O Israel: The *Lord* our God, the *Lord* is one" (6:4). For the word translated *Lord* in this verse Moses uses Yahweh/Jehovah. This name bears such holiness that the people of Israel did not pronounce it verbally, and when written, it required the use of a special pen. The people of Israel held this name in such sanctity that they would never use it for anyone else.

However, the prophet Jeremiah later used this same name, Yahweh/Jehovah, to describe the future Messiah—Jesus. He stated,

"In his days Judah will be saved and Israel will live in safety. This is the name by which he will be called: The *Lord* Our Righteousness" (Jeremiah 23:6). Furthermore, the prophet Ezekiel referred to the Holy Spirit with this same holy name. He stated,

> In the sixth year, in the sixth month on the fifth day, while I was sitting in my house and the elders of Judah were sitting before me, the hand of the Sovereign *Lord* came on men there. I looked, and I saw a figure like that of a man. From what appeared to be his waist down he was like fire, and from there up his appearance was as bright as glowing metal. He stretched out what looked like a hand and took me by the hair of my head. The Spirit lifted me up between earth and heaven and in visions of God he took me to Jerusalem, to the entrance of the north gate of the inner court, where the idol that provokes to jealousy stood (Ezekiel 8:1-3).

So, Moses referred to the Father as Yahweh/Jehovah. Jeremiah also applied the same name to the Messiah, Jesus the Son. Ezekiel used the same name to refer to the Holy Spirit. These three examples merely offer a sample of the Hebrew mindset that God the Father, the Messiah (the Son), and the Holy Spirit constitute one and the same God, not three. The fact that they use the most holy name of God, Yahweh/Jehovah, for all three persons demonstrates an internalized understanding of the Trinity in the Old Testament.

The New Testament

The name Yahweh/Jehovah does not appear in the New Testament, since it comes from Hebrew, and the New Testament authors wrote in Koiné Greek. However, Rabbinic Jewish scholars translated the Old Testament into Koiné Greek centuries before Jesus' birth in a text called the Septuagint. In fact, studies show that several New Testament authors, and Jesus himself quoted the Septuagint translation when they cited the Old Testament. The connections between the Septuagint, and the New Testament show that Yahweh/Jehovah in Hebrew is the same as the Greek word, *kurios*, meaning supreme authority, master, or *Lord*. In the New Testament, when individuals used *kurios* to refer to God, they implied that God has no one equal to him, or above him. Old Testament individuals used the name Yahweh/Jehovah with equal weight in reference to each person of the Trinity (Martin, Brook and Duncan, 1992, 112).

Jesus used *kurios* to refer to the Father when he stated, "I praise you, Father, *Lord* of heaven and earth, because you have hidden these things from the wise and learned, and revealed them to little children" (Matthew 11:25). The angel who spoke to Mary when she was pregnant with Jesus called him Christ (the New Testament term for Messiah) the *Lord* and used this same term stating, "Today in the town of David a Savior has been born to you; he is the Messiah, the *Lord*." (Luke 2:11). Paul also used *kurios* to refer to the Holy Spirit, stating, "Now the *Lord* is the Spirit, and where the Spirit of the *Lord* is, there is freedom." (2 Corinthians 3:17).

Therefore, *kurios* does not only describe the Father, according to Jesus, but according to the angels, it also describes the Son—Jesus, and according to Paul, *kurios* also describes the Holy Spirit. Consequently, in the minds of the New Testament people, God exists in three persons, but still one and the same God. The concept of the Trinity did not come as something new to the New Testament people, but rather something that their culture understood—that the Father, the Son, and the Holy Spirit all exist as someone, not something, personal and unified in the Trinity.

Holy Spirit's Personality

Some people look at the previous references of Scripture that use God's name, or title of *Lord* to the Holy Spirit as just another aspect of God the Father. However, Scripture clearly demonstrates that the Holy Spirit does not comprise part of God, nor does he exist as a manifestation of his power, or influence. The Holy Spirit possesses his own function and personality distinct from the Father and the Son.

In the creation of the world, the Father had as specific job, he spoke the world into creation (Genesis 1:3, 6, 9, 11, 14, 20, 24).

Jesus the Son, had a separate job; he did the creating (John 1:1-3; Colossians 1:16). The Holy Spirit also had his own function, to witness to the process of the creation (Genesis 1:2). As the witness, this testimony allows the Holy Spirit to later inspire the authors of the Bible (2 Timothy 3:16).

In the New Testament era, the Holy Spirit focused the attention on Jesus Christ and glorified him (John 15:26; 16:14). Therefore, the person of Holy Spirit is separate from the Father and the Son, yet still exists in union with them as one God.

The Bible explicitly evokes the discernable person of the Holy Spirit (Romans 8:27; 1 Corinthians 2:10-11); who possesses wisdom, intelligence, emotions, and a will (Isaiah 11:2; Ephesians 1:17; 4:30; Romans 8:5; Galatians 5:16-17). Inanimate objects cannot possess any of these traits, rather someone must possess them. This brings us back to the understanding that the Holy Spirit is a "who", not a "what".

The Holy Spirit's Function for the Church

Once we understand the "who" of the Holy Spirit, we can then begin to understand what he does for the Church. Within the Trinitarian relationship, the Father sent the Son (John 20:21), the Son sent the Spirit (John 14:16), and the Holy Spirits gives the empowering gifts to fulfill the Great Commission (1 Corinthians 12:1-11; Acts 1:8; Matthew 28:19-20; Mark 16:15).

We should also understand that Jesus did not act in his divine power, but rather in the power of the Holy Spirit (Luke 4:18). Jesus' dependence on the Holy Spirit as the source of power to fulfill his ministry allowed him to say, ". . .whoever believes in me will do the works I have been doing, and they will do even greater things than these. . ." (John 14:12).

Therefore, the Holy Spirit's function for the Church helps followers of Jesus to fulfill their call to ministry, and their part in the Great Commission. When Jesus commanded his teenage disciples to make disciples of all nations and preach the Gospel to all creation, he asked them to fulfill an impossible task, so he sent the

Holy Spirit. Jesus' last words did not come as a coincidence. "You will receive power when the Holy Spirit comes on you. . ." (Acts 1:8a). Then Jesus stated the why, "and you will be my witnesses in Jerusalem, and in all Judea and Samaria, and to the ends of the earth" (v. 8b). Jesus never expected his disciples to fulfill an impossible task without sending someone to empower them with the tools to complete the job.

We can see the evidence of the tools the Holy Spirit gives us throughout the whole Bible. God demonstrated a pattern in both testaments so believers can know that the Spirit has filled them with the power to do their part in the Great Commission. The next chapter explores this pattern in the Old Testament.

Part II

The Filling of the Holy Spirit in the Old Covenant

MANY BOOKS THAT DISCUSS the Holy Spirit, or the work of the Holy Spirit focus on the New Testament. However, if we are to understand how the Holy Spirit works, we cannot begin in the middle of the story, we need to start from the beginning. So, in this section I want to take you on a journey from the beginning of the Bible. Here we will see the pattern of how the Holy Spirit has always worked when empowering people. This pattern will later help us understand why things happened the way they happened in the New Testament, in Church history, and for us today.

Chapter 2

The Old Testament Experience

Introduction

DID YOU KNOW THAT in the Old Testament, virtually every time the Holy Spirit comes on, fills, lifts, or does something similar to an individual, the initial evidence of that experience came in some sort of prophetic form? Many people understand prophecy as foretelling what will happen. Such experiences can take on a prophetic nature, but only partially describe prophecy. Prophecy is a very broad and simple concept. It consists of written or verbal communication inspired by God. Consequently, with this definition, the Bible itself constitutes prophecy, "All Scripture is God-breathed, and is useful for teaching, rebuking, correcting and training in righteousness" (2 Timothy 3:16a). When an individual spoke for God, he prophesied. When individuals today use the communication gifts of the Spirit: messages of wisdom or knowledge, general prophecy, tongues, and interpretation of tongues, which the Holy Spirit imparted in the New Testament, they also prophesy (ref. 1 Corinthians 12:8, 10). Now that we understand prophecy, we can understand how it links to the work of the Holy Spirit in the Old Testament. This chapter outlines the pattern of Spirit-inspired speech and its connection to the work of the Holy Spirit.

The Patriarchal Era

Elihu, Job's Young Friend (Job 32)

Many theologians agree that the book of Job chronologically predates any other book in the Bible. While Job may not record the earliest events that Moses recorded in Genesis, the evidence found in units of measurement, and other inferences imply that the author of Job wrote the book between the time of the patriarchs (Abraham) and Moses. Therefore, we begin with the oldest recorded movement of the Holy Spirit in the Bible.

The majority of the book of Job is a conversation between Job and God, and Job and his three friends. However, toward the end of the book, Job's three friends give up on him, and another younger friend, Elihu, enters the scene. Elihu had held back in the shadows of the conversation but in chapter 32, he finally spoke out. He clarified that his prophetic speech came from the inspiration of the Holy Spirit stating, "For I am full of words, and the spirit within me compels me; inside I am like bottled-up wine, like new wineskins ready to burst. I must speak and find relief; I must open my lips and reply. I will show no partiality, nor will I flatter anyone; for if I were skilled in flattery, my Maker would soon take me away" (vv. 18-22).

It should not surprise the us that this filling of the Holy Spirit resulted in a prophetic outburst. We can also find comfort in knowing that after a long conversation throughout most of the book of Job, Elihu's speech constitutes the first true utterance of wisdom from one of Job's friends. Therefore, the Bible connects its oldest record of a filling of the Holy Spirit with prophecy.

Moses and the Seventy-two Elders (Numbers 11)

Moses recorded an argument with the Lord in Numbers about how to feed all of the Israelites that he led in the dessert. After hearing from the Lord he brought together seventy of their elders and had them stand around the tent of meeting where the Ark of the Covenant rested. "Then the Lord came down in the cloud and spoke with him, and he took some of the power of the Spirit that was on him and put it on the seventy elders. When the Spirit rested on them, they prophesied—but did not do so again" (v. 25).

Similar to the Elihu record, when the Spirit rested on the seventy elders, their initial response came in the form of prophecy. This verse also states that the Spirit rested on Moses, and the Bible considered Moses as the greatest prophet until Jesus (ref. Deuteronomy 34:10; Hebrews 3:1-6).

When the Spirit descended upon the seventy elders, two others had come in to such close proximity that ". . .the Spirit also rested on them, and they prophesied in the camp" (v. 26b). This experience demonstrated the third time the Holy Spirit filled someone; thus, establishing a biblical pattern.

Interestingly, jealousy grew in Moses' followers because these two individuals also prophesied, but were not among the seventy elders. However, Moses' response reflected a greater interest when he expressed his desire, "I wish that all the Lord's people were prophets and that the Lord would put his Spirit on them!" (v. 29b). Moses articulated a desire for God to pour out this prophetic experience on all of his people. We will later see that desire develop into a prophecy by Joel, and fulfilled on the day of Pentecost.

Jewish tradition also provides an interesting edition to Moses' prophetic accounts in the Midrash[1]. This ancient Jewish text provides insight into the episode when Moses gave the law written on the Ten Commandments (Exodus 20:18-21). In the Midrash, Exodus Rabbah 5:9[2] stated. . .

> When God gave the Torah[3] on Sinai He displayed untold
> marvels to Israel with his voice. What happened? God

1. The Midrash is a rabbinical commentary on the Scriptures written around the eleventh century

2. Exodus Rabbah is the Jewish commentary on the Midrash from the book of Exodus in the Bible.

3. *Torah* means "law" and it began with the Ten Commandments. The law was later expanded to include the first five books of the Bible, the writings of Moses, and what we call the Pentateuch.

spoke and the voice reverberated throughout the whole world. . . It says, and all the people witnessed the thundering's. God's voice, as it was uttered split up into seventy voices, in seventy languages, so that all the nations should understand.

Due to the fact that this account comes from outside the Bible, we cannot accept it with the same weight as Scripture. However, we cannot ignore this provocative evidence of ancient Jewish tradition either.

Balaam's Prophecy (Numbers 24)

Shortly after the prophetic episode with Moses and the seventy-two elders, the Israelites found themselves near Moab. The Moabite king, Balak, offered to pay a diviner named Balaam to prophesy against Israel, but "When Balaam looked out and saw Israel encamped tribe by tribe, the Spirit of God came on him and he spoke his message. . ." (vv. 2-3). The rest of the chapter consists of five prophetic messages from Balaam in favor of Israel instead of against. Balaam's prophecies resulted as a connection to the filling of the Spirit.

This prophetic episode relates to our study for two reasons: 1. It continues the biblical pattern of the filling of the Holy Spirit and prophetic utterance, and 2. It constitutes the first record of the Holy Spirit filling a Gentile (a non-Hebrew) who also happened to prophesy even though he didn't follow God. Balaam's prophetic experience demonstrated that the Spirit can use whomever he wishes to carry his message and fulfill his will.

The Judicial Era

The Judges

After Moses' leadership and the entrance into the Promised Land of Canaan, God raised up prophets who served as judges or chieftains. These men and women primarily served their local tribe in

Israel and held places of leadership because they heard from the Lord. The author of the Book of Judges intentionally mentioned the Holy Spirit's involvement in their prophetic utterances. Old Testament theologian, J. Barton Payne evokes this prophetic notion stating: . . .

> God did, however, raise up Joshua and certain priests, judges, and Nazarites as "charismatic" leaders to deliver Israel. Such men—and women—were specially filled by the *charism*, or gift, God's Holy Spirit (Judg. 6:34), whose personal activity comes to the forefront in this period. But the most significant feature of the consolidation period lies in the development of Biblical prophecy into its second major stage, namely, the rise of the prophets into an organized class for regular use by God (Payne 1962, 49).

Othniel rose up as the first of twelve judges listed in the book of Judges (3:7-13). The author intentionally stated that "The Spirit of the Lord came upon him, so that he became Israel's judge" (v. 10). The fact that the judges also served as prophets continues the biblical pattern of the connection of the filling of the Holy Spirit and Othniel's prophetic position as a judge over Israel.

Similarly, when Gideon came into his prophetic office as a judge, the author of the book noted at the beginning of his ministry, "Then the Spirit of the Lord came upon Gideon, and he blew a trumpet, summoning the Abiezrites to follow him. He sent messages throughout Manasseh. . ." (6:34-35a). The initial response when the Spirit came upon Gideon originated in the form of Spirit-inspired communication. God used Gideon to communicate a message to the rest of Israel to raise an army and gain their freedom from the Philistines. Therefore, the communication in Gideon's trumpet, and the message he sent falls under the definition of prophecy.

Jephthah's story as a judge has a peculiar development because he was the son of a prostitute (ref. 11:1). Regardless of his background, God raised Jephthah up as one of his Judges of Israel (ref. 11:11). Judges recorded that "the Spirit of the Lord came upon Jephthah" (11:29), and the first thing that came out of his mouth in the biblical record is a vow to God (11:30). It is interesting to think that after the Holy Spirit came upon Jephthah, his initial response is a vow of dedication to the Lord.

Samson's story stands out as the most famous of the judges. Though the record uniquely differs for this biblical superhero, we must remember that all of the judges were not only leaders, but they were also prophets. When Samson stepped into leadership as a judge of Israel, the author of Judges linked his prophetic office to his leadership stating, "and the Spirit of the Lord began to stir him. . ." (13:25). Here, the filling of the Holy Spirit initiated Samson as prophet/judge.

Some may argue that Judges contains three more records where the Holy Spirit came upon Samson, and they reference a feat of strength rather than a prophetic utterance (14:6; 19; 15:14). However, we cannot forget that Samson's career as judge and prophet began with the filling of the Holy Spirit. Samson's feats of strength only reinforce the notion that the Holy Spirit empowered him to fulfill his task for the Lord, just as the Holy Spirit empowered the early church to fulfill its task for the Lord (ref. Acts 1:8). The Book of Judges continued the biblical pattern of prophecy when the Holy Spirit came upon individuals. Walter Kaiser notes that: . . .

> The purpose of Judges is to demonstrate that 'in those days Israel had no king; everyone did as he saw fit (Judges 17:6; 21:25; cf. 18:1; 19:1). The period of the judges stressed the charismatic leadership under the working of the Holy Spirit. One ruler (here also called a 'judge') after another was raised up and anointed in response to the people's exhaustion with their sin and disobedience (Kaiser 2008, 102).

Therefore, all twelve of the judges in this book served as prophets carrying a Spirit-inspired message to bring the people of Israel back to serve the Lord. This prophetic pattern created a bridge from the patriarchal period of Job and Moses, through the pre-monarchial period of the judges to Israel's first king—Saul.

The Monarchial Era

Saul Anointed as King (1 Samuel 10)

As a young man, Saul and a servant went looking for his father's lost donkeys. They ended up at the prophet Samuel's home to find help locating the donkeys. Unexpectedly, Samuel anointed Saul to become the first king of Israel. At that time Samuel told Saul that when he left, he would meet a group of prophets and, "The Spirit of the Lord will come upon you in power, and you will prophesy with them and you will be changed into a different person" (v. 6). When Saul left all the things Samuel had foretold came to pass (ref. vv. 10-14).

The rise of King Saul began a new era in the history of Israel. With this new era, the biblical pattern continued with the connection of the Holy Spirit coming upon this new ruler and his prophetic utterance. King Saul's prophetic experience served as a bridge from the period of the judges to this new era of monarch rule in Israel.

David, the Future King of Israel (1 Samuel 16 & 2 Samuel 23)

When Samuel established David's dynasty, he "took the horn of oil and anointed him in the presence of his brothers, and from that day on the Spirit of the Lord came upon David in power" (v. 13). David's anointing signified the beginning of a new dynasty that would last forever (2 Samuel 17:12-16). Although David did not prophesy when Samuel anointed him, prophecy inundated David's reign throughout the Psalms. The biblical record states that the Spirit of the Lord came upon David when Samuel first anointed him as king, and he experienced prophetic utterance throughout his life. In fact, David prophesied with his last words before he died declaring, "The Spirit of the Lord spoke through me: his word was on my tongue" (2 Samuel 23:2). The life and rule of King David continued the biblical pattern of the connection between the filling of the Holy Spirit and prophecy.

King Saul and His Men (1 Samuel 19)

With the rise of David's popularity, and the fact that the prophet Samuel had anointed David as the next king (1 Samuel 16:1-13), Saul grew jealous of David. Unexpectedly, when Saul sent his soldiers to capture David, they came upon a company of prophets and Samuel where, "the Spirit of God came upon Saul's men and they also prophesied. When Saul's men told him what happened, he sent more men, and they prophesied too. Saul sent men a third time and they also prophesied" (vv. 20-21). On three separate occasions, when Saul's soldiers came near Samuel's company of prophets, they could not resist the filling of the Holy Spirit and their initial response in every occasion came as prophecy.

The divine response of Saul's men enraged him, so he went himself to capture David. Yet again, as when he first found himself among Samuel's company of prophets, "the Spirit of God came even upon him, and he walked along prophesying until he came to Naioth. He stripped off his robes and also prophesied in Samuel's presence. He lay that way all the day and night. This is why people say, 'Is Saul also among the prophets?'" (vv. 23-24). Therefore, at the beginning, and at the end of King Saul's reign, the biblical pattern continued with the connection of filling of the Holy Spirit and prophetic utterance.

Elijah Challenges King Ahab (1 Kings 18)

Nearly two centuries after King Saul, Queen Jezebel killed most off God's prophets in the kingdom of Israel. One of the last prophets, Elijah, boldly presented himself to Obadiah, one of King Ahab's servants. Obadiah replied, "I don't know where the Spirit of the Lord may carry you when I leave you. . ." (v. 12). Obadiah's response reflected the fact that the Holy Spirit had descended upon

Elijah, and if Elijah's reputation as a prophet came lacking, in this same chapter, Elijah prophesied against the false prophets of Baal on Mount Carmel. The significance of this episode further notes the continued connection between prophecy and the action of the Holy Spirit.

Micaiah's Prophesy against King Ahab (1 Kings 22)

After Elijah prophesied before King Ahab and destroyed the false prophets, King Jehoshaphat of Judah went to King Ahab of Israel to discuss going to war against the king of Aram. They looked for a prophet to hear from the Lord before preparing for battle. The kings summoned the unpopular prophet Micaiah. As he prophesied, Micaiah foretold of Judah and Israel's failure, and Ahab's death. "Then Zedekiah son of Kenaanah went up and slapped Micaiah in the face. 'Which way did the spirit from the Lord go when he went from me to speak to you?' he asked" (v. 24).

Although Zedekiah's insult of Micaiah reflects sarcasm, the biblical record reveals that the Holy Spirit had descended upon Micaiah, and his prophecies, though unpopular, were Spirit-inspired. The rest of chapter reveals more prophetic utterance from Micaiah, and the fulfillment of those prophecies. This episode discloses the continuation of the biblical pattern of the connection between the filling of the Holy Spirit and prophecy during the period of the divided kingdom in Israel.

Jahaziel the Levite Prophesied to King Jehoshaphat (2 Chronicles 20)

At the same time Micaiah prophesied against King Ahab of Israel, "the Spirit of the Lord came upon Jahaziel" (v. 14a). The following verses (vv. 15-18) record the initial response to the coming of the Holy Spirit was prophecy, which comes to pass in favor of King Jehoshaphat of Judah in the rest of the chapter. The significance of this biblical record notes the continued connection between the coming of the Holy Spirit and prophetic utterance during the period of the divided kingdom, but in Judah.

Joel Prophesies Moses' Desire (Joel 2)

Roughly seven centuries after Moses expressed his desire, "I wish that all the Lord's people were prophets and that the Lord would put his Spirit on them!" (Numbers 11:29b); Joel prophesied that this would actually come to pass. Speaking for the Lord, Joel stated. . .

> And afterward, I will pour out my Spirit on all people. Your sons and daughters will prophesy, your old men will dream dreams, you young men will see visions. Even on my servants, both men and women, I will pour out my Spirit in those days. I will show wonders in the heavens, and on the earth, blood and fire and billows of smoke. The sun will be turned to darkness and the moon to blood before the coming of the great and dreadful day of the Lord. And everyone who calls on the name of the Lord will be saved, for on Mount Zion and in Jerusalem there will be deliverance, as the Lord has said, among the survivors whom the Lord calls (Joel 2:28-32).

Until this point in history, prophetic utterances came as isolated incidents, not continuous. However, the all-inclusive language of Joel's prophecy revealed that God planned to eventually open continual prophetic access to all people, both young and old, slave and free, male and female. In Acts 2:16-21, the Apostle Peter cites this passage as the beginning of the fulfillment of this prophecy. Joel's prophecy explicitly connected the move of the Holy Spirit and its prophetic evidence in the Old Testament with the baptism in the Holy Spirit, and the initial evidence in the prophetic gift of speaking in tongues as on the day of Pentecost.

Isaiah's Prophetic Call (Isaiah 6)

In 740 B.C., "the year that King Uzziah died" (v. 1), God called Isaiah to a prophetic ministry. In his humanity, Isaiah recognized his unworthiness stating, "'Woe to me!' I cried. 'I am ruined! For I am a man of unclean lips, and I live among a people of unclean lips, and my eyes have seen the King, the Lord Almighty'" (v. 5). Isaiah connected his commission and the confirmation of his prophetic office with his mouth. He stated, "I am a man of unclean lips," therefore, God purified Isaiah through his mouth (v. 5). So "one of the seraphs flew to [him] with a live coal in his hand, which he had taken with tongs from the altar. With it he touched [Isaiah's] mouth and said, 'See, this has touched your lips; your guilt is taken away and your sin atoned for'" (vv. 6-7). God moved through an angel, preparing Isaiah's mouth to be used in service as a prophet.

Ezekiel's Prophetic Career (Ezekiel 11)

During Ezekiel's prophetic career, "the Spirit lifted him up" (v. 1), and he prophesied (v. 4). Later, "the Spirit of the Lord came upon him" and he prophesied (v. 5). The rest of this chapter continues with that prophecy. Ezekiel's prophetic experience followed the biblical pattern of the initial evidence of prophecy after the move of the Holy Spirit.

Micah's Prophecy Against the False Prophets of Israel (Micah 3)

During the time that Isaiah prophesied to the kings of Judah, Micah was also prophesying to the kings of Israel. He stated, "But as for me, I am filled with power, with the Spirit of the Lord" (v. 8). Immediately after his declaration, Micah prophesied to the leadership of Israel rebuking them for listening to false prophets, seeking their own selfish gain, and claiming that they were being used by God (vv. 9-12).

Conclusion

In every major period of the Old Testament, patriarchal, judicial, and monarchial, from when God began to use people to speak for him, the biblical record demonstrates a continuous pattern with a connection between the move of the Holy Spirit and prophecy. These observations demonstrate that this connection does not merely constitute a list of descriptive passages. Rather it displays a pattern of how God works though his Holy Spirit and the evidence of how he moves in humanity in a prophetic way.

Chapter 3

The Old Testament Experience in The New Testament

Introduction

AFTER THE FALL OF the Kingdoms of Israel (722 B.C.) and Judah (586 B.C.), the last of the prophets, such as Haggai, Zechariah, and Malachi began to prophesy (in the fifth century B.C.). From that point in history, and during the following four centuries, the Persians, the Greeks, and the Romans conquered the biblical lands. However, this era still experienced the continuation of the prophetic gift. This chapter addresses the continuation of the biblical pattern of the move of the Holy Spirit and its connection to the gift of prophesy in the period between the Old and New Testaments.

The Intertestamental Period: After the Old Testament Prophets to the Birth of Christ

Rabbinic tradition suggests that the filling of the Holy Spirit and prophecy continued during the period between the Old and New Testaments. The ancient Jewish writing *Tosefta Sotah* (8:2),[1] refers to the fact that "When the last prophets, Haggai, Zechariah, and

---

1. The *Tosefta Sotah* is a book of rabbinic traditions from the second century A.D.

Malachi, died, the Holy Spirit ceased out of Israel; but neverthe-less it was granted them to hear (communications from God) by means of a mysterious voice" (Foot Moore 1971, 124). This refer-ence gives an illusion to prophecy during this era, because people continued to hear from God.

During the second century B.C., from the revolts sparked by Judas Maccabeus, Josephus recorded in the *Jewish War* that the new leadership under the Hasmonean dynasty encompassed men with the gift of prophecy (8:2-15).

Due to the period in which these historic events took place, between the last prophets of the Old Testament and the events re-corded in the gospels, the Bible has no record of them. Therefore, we cannot accept these accounts with the same certainty of the Bible. However, we can neither ignore that several historical sourc-es have survived recording prophecies during the intertestamental period. If these events truly did come to pass, they would serve as evidence to the continuation of prophecy during a biblically silent time.

The A.D. Period: From the Birth of Christ to the Crucifixion

The terms "testament" and "covenant" are synonyms, describing one another. Even though the New Testament includes the four Gospels of Matthew, Mark, Luke, and John, the events recorded in these Gospels fall under the law of the covenant in the Old Tes-tament. Therefore, God continued to follow the same pattern as in the Old Testament because Jesus had not yet fulfilled the law (Matthew 5:17-18) in order to make a new covenant by dying on the cross (Jeremiah 31:31-34; Hebrews 9:15). Only after the cruci-fixion does the veil of the Holy of Holies in the temple tear in two from top to bottom (Matthew 27:50-51). From that moment, the law was fulfilled and the covenant of the New Testament began.

In light of the old covenant Luke intentionally mentioned six people in the first four chapters of his gospel who were filled with the Holy Spirit. Luke further mentioned that they also prophesied, continuing the biblical pattern set in the Old Testament. This chapter focuses on those six people: (1) Elizabeth the mother of John the Baptist; (2) Mary the mother of Jesus; (3) Zechariah the father of John the Baptist; (4) Simeon the elderly man in the temple; (5) John the Baptist; and (6) Jesus.

Elizabeth, John the Baptist's Mother (Luke 1)

After becoming pregnant with Jesus through the power of the Holy Spirit (v. 35), Mary went to her cousin, Elizabeth's, house in the country and. . .

> When Elizabeth heard Mary's greeting, the baby leaped in her womb, and Elizabeth was filled with the Holy Spirit. In a loud voice she exclaimed: "Blessed are you among women, and blessed is the child you will bear! But why am I so favored, that the mother of my Lord should come to me? As soon as the sound of your greeting reached my ears, the baby in my womb leaped for joy. Blessed is she who has believed that the Lord would fulfill his promises to her!" (vv. 41-45).

In this statement, Elizabeth prophesied about the future Messiah in her cousin, Mary's, womb. From his first chapter Luke intentionally mentioned that the Holy Spirit had filled Elizabeth, followed by prophetic expression. So, from the beginning of the Gospel a connection exists between the biblical pattern of prophecy as the initial experience of the filling of the Holy Spirit.

Mary, Jesus' Mother (Luke 1)

The biblical record notes that Mary was full of the Spirit when she became pregnant with Jesus (Matthew 1:18; Luke 1:35). After visiting her cousin, Elizabeth, in the countryside, Luke recorded Mary's song. Mothers normally sing to their babies even before they give birth. So we must ask, why did Luke record this song from Mary? (vv. 46-55). By reading the content of the song, similar to Hannah's song (1 Samuel 2:1-10), we can see that its prophetic in nature. Therefore, Luke continues to mention prophecy in connection to the filling of the Holy Spirit.

Zechariah, John the Baptist's Father (Luke 1)

We find the third account of the filling of the Holy Spirit in the same chapter with the priest and father of John the Baptist, Zechariah. Verses 11-20 explain that while Zechariah burned incense in the temple, the angel Gabriel appeared to him and said that he would have a son, and that the son would become a prophet. Gabriel further explained that this son would go before the Lord in the spirit and power of Elijah, and that Zechariah must name him John. However, due to Zechariah's initial unbelief, he remained unable to speak until his son's birth.

After Elizabeth gave birth to John, Zechariah could speak. He announced his son's name—John, delivering Gabriel's message who delivered God's message. Therefore, Zechariah's initial expression came as prophesy inspired by God (vv. 51-66). Shortly after this event, Luke wrote, "His father Zechariah was filled with the Holy Spirit and prophesied:" (v. 67). Then Zechariah's prophetic song follows (vv. 68-79), similar to Mary's prophetic song. Luke begins his gospel explicitly connecting prophecy and the filling of the Spirit. Theologian Roger Stronstad puts it this way, "'Filled with the Holy Spirit' is the introductory formula, and the direct speech which follows is a *pneuma* discourse, that is, prophecy inspired by the Spirit" (2010, 62).

Simeon, the Old Man in the Temple (Luke 2)

When Jesus was a baby, only eight days old, his parents took him to the temple to be circumcised (vv. 21-24).

> Now there was a man in Jerusalem called Simeon, who was righteous and devout. He was waiting for the consolation of Israel, and the Holy Spirit was on him. It had

been revealed to him by the Holy Spirit that he would not die before he had seen the Lord's Messiah. Moved by the Spirit, he went into the temple courts. When the parents brought in the child Jesus to do for him what the custom of the law required, Simeon took him in his arms and praised God (vv. 25-28).

As the Holy Spirit moved Simeon, his immediate expression as he took the baby Jesus in his arms came as prophecy (v. 29-32), and "The child's father and mother marveled at what was said about him" (v. 33). Simeon continued speaking with Mary prophesying even more stating, "This child is destined to cause the falling and rising of many in Israel, and to be a sign that will be spoken against, so that the thoughts of many hearts will be revealed. And a sword will pierce your own soul too" (vv. 34b-35). Yet again, Luke evoked the account of Simeon, thus demonstrating the continuation of the biblical pattern of the connection between the filling of the Holy Spirit and prophecy.

John the Baptist (Luke 3)

John the Baptist "[was] *filled with the Holy Spirit* even from birth" (Luke 1:15). Therefore, he served as a prophet who "[went] before the Lord, in the Spirit and power of Elijah" (Luke 1:17). Jesus also declared that John the Baptist fulfilled the prophecy of Elijah's return (Malachi 4:5-6; Matthew 11:4; 17:10-13). John himself fulfilled this prophecy foretelling Jesus' ministry as the "voice of one calling in the desert, 'Prepare the way for the Lord, make straight paths for him. . .'" (Luke 3:1-6; Isaiah 40:3-5; Malachi 3:1). John was not just any prophet. Jesus held him in high esteem stating, "among those born of women there has not risen anyone greater than John the Baptist" (Matthew 11:11). Therefore, John, full of the Holy Spirit from birth and confirmed as a prophet (Luke 3), demonstrated a strong connection between the filling of the Holy Spirit and prophecy.

Jesus' Prophetic and Empowered Ministry (Luke 4)

Jesus never exercised his own divine power, rather he worked "in the power of the Spirit" (v. 14). Even though Jesus, in his ministry on Earth, lived completely as God and completely as man simultaneously, he always depended on the power of the Holy Spirit. This explains why Jesus sent the Holy Spirit to empower believers (John 14:15-17; 20:21; Acts 1:8); and why Jesus could say, "Very truly I tell you, whoever believes in me will do the works I have been doing, and they will do even greater things than these" (John 14:12). So, Jesus submitted himself to the same biblical pattern as the rest of humanity expressing that we base our dependence on the power of the Holy Spirit.

Many people ask, if the gift of tongues constitutes the initial evidence of the baptism in the Holy Spirit, then why didn't Jesus speak in tongues? In light of the biblical pattern of the Old Testament, general prophecy constituted the initial evidence of the filling of the Holy Spirit.

The life of Christ took place under the covenant of the Old Testament since he had no yet fulfilled the law on the cross, spilling his blood. Therefore, he came under the same biblical pattern as the people of the Old Testament. Consequently, Jesus only prophesied; however, we could argue that everything Jesus said was prophecy, because he communicated directly as God. Thus the author of Hebrews elevated Jesus as a greater prophet than Moses (3:1-6). Jesus even identified himself as a prophet (Matthew 21:11) and the people also identified him as such (Luke 4:24).

Conclusion

Luke uniquely mentions these six main characters in the beginning of his gospel. As a physician, Dr. Luke paid a great deal of attention to detail, and as a good historian, "[he had] carefully investigated everything from the beginning, (and had decided) to write an orderly account" (Luke 1:3). Luke not only strove to relay the history Jesus' life and ministry to the gentile official, Theophilus; Luke also intended to teach him. Therefore, Luke didn't write about everything; rather, he chose specific events, focusing on the Holy Spirit more than his synoptic colleagues. For example, Mark mentioned the Holy Spirit six times, and Matthew mentioned him twelve, but Luke mentioned the Holy Spirit seventeen times, with a greater focus on the Holy Spirit.

Theologian Howard Marshall suggested that these events confirm Luke as a trustworthy historian and a theologian of the first rank (Marshall 1970). Theologians William and Robert Menzies concur, "Luke-Acts represents history with a purpose—history written with a theological agenda in view" (Menzies and Menzies 2000, 41). Roger Stronstad confirms this notion declaring, "Luke had a didactic or catechetical or instructional, rather than a merely informational, purpose for his history of the origin and spread of Christianity" (Stronstad 2005, 51).

Therefore, we can see that the events between the Old and New Testaments, and the events at the beginning of Christ's life and ministry follow the biblical pattern of the filling of the Holy Spirit and subsequent prophecy. However, Luke demonstrates that connection not merely as normal, but as normative. In the next chapter we will see this point brought to light even more so during the New Testament era.

Part III

The Filling of the Holy Spirit in the New Covenant

THE AGE OF THE early church in the New Testament expanded from the time of the crucifixion (approximately A.D. 33), until the end of the first century. The Church was born during this period along with the twenty-seven books of the New Testament. This era also saw the experience of the filling of the Holy Spirit and a significant change in human history.

From the age of the Old Testament patriarchs until the Day of Pentecost in Acts 2, when the Holy Spirit filled an individual, their initial response took the form of prophetic expression. We must also remember that communication inspired by God either in written or verbal form defines prophecy.

However, in the New Testament, John the Baptist expresses that things were changing. Thus John fulfills the voice calling in the wilderness to prepare the way for the Lord (Isaiah 40:3; Malachi 3:1; Matthew 3:3; Mark 1:3; Luke 3:4; John 1:23). John expressed that this change would come in the form of a baptism by fire and the Holy Spirit (Matthew 3:11; Mark 1:8; Luke 3:16; John 1:26). Consequently, John coined the unique term "baptism" in the Holy Spirit in order to connect it to his baptism ministry, and to the Holy Spirit's operation in the Old Testament when the Holy Spirit came on an individual.

Acts encompasses a significant portion of the history of the early church. Acts also focuses on the move of the Holy Spirit during that time. So in this chapter we focus on Luke's account in the book of Acts. We'll see the continuation of the biblical pattern of the connection between the filling of the Holy Spirit and prophecy. However, in this time period, under the new covenant, three major distinctions exist. Frist, tongues comes as a unique form of prophecy. Secondly, prophecy does not occur in isolated events like in the Old Testament, rather it occurs continuously. Thirdly, this experience does not happen solely to prophets, rather the Spirit opens his experience to all believers as a normative (an expectation) practice for followers of Christ.

Many perspectives exist about the baptism in the Holy Spirit; however, two specific perspectives stand out. One view looks at the events of the filling of the Holy Spirit through the lens of Paul. On the other hand, a different perspective looks at the events through the lens of Luke. Individuals from both perspectives often error because they interpret Luke's words using verses that Paul wrote, and vice versa, interpreting Paul's words using verses that Luke wrote. William and Robert Menzies illuminate this issue stating, "Paul frequently speaks of the soteriological dimension of the Spirit's work (the Holy Spirit in salvation), Luke consistently portrays the Spirit as the source of power for service" (Menzies and Menzies 2000, 50). Therefore, we must interpret Luke using Luke, and Paul using Paul. This section deals with each of these biblical authors to understand their unique perspectives in light of the move of the Holy Spirit and its evidence.

Chapter 4

What Did Luke Say?

Introduction

LUKE WROTE BOTH OF his books to an audience of one, a man named Theophilus, likely a Greek or Roman official, but certainly not a Jew. Therefore, the audience of Luke and Acts knew nothing of the filling of the Spirit in the Old Testament. Luke did not merely write a general history of the life and ministry of Christ and the Church; rather he taught Theophilus what Christianity is. Roger Stronstad dedicates his book, *The Charismatic Theology of St. Luke* to validate Luke as a theologian and that his books, Luke and Acts, primarily teach Theophilus about the move of the Holy Spirit (1984).

The full name of Luke's second book, *The Acts of the Apostles,* may seem curious, because other than Peter, John, Philip, Andrew, and Paul, Luke does not mention the acts of the other apostles. The primary focus of Acts deals with Peter and Paul; however, the Holy Spirit is actually Luke's main character. Luke did not merely give a historical account, rather he focused on specific events. Luke avoided other historical events suggesting that the book of Acts is not really a history, but rather a didactic narrative (that is to say, he wanted to teach Theophilus something specific).

Luke begins Acts with Jesus' last words to his disciples stating, "you will receive power when the Holy Spirit comes on you; and you will be my witnesses in Jerusalem, and in all Judea and Samaria, and to the ends of the earth" (Acts 1:8). This famous verse demonstrates how the Holy Spirit moved through the disciples. Luke also used this verse to teach Theophilus that the purpose of the baptism experience is to empower people to be witnesses for Christ, fulfilling the Great Commission. So, let's take a look at how this played out through the book of Acts.

The Baptism at Pentecost (Acts 2)

According to Jesus' in Acts 1:8, on the Day of Pentecost the baptism in the Holy Spirit began in Jerusalem. The word "Pentecost" comes from the Greek *Pentēcostē*, meaning "fiftieth". Pentecost began as a Jewish feast that took place fifty days after Passover. In the Old Testament they called it the "Feast of Weeks" because it represented seven sevens, or seven weeks—fulfillment, perfection, a time of times. According to rabbinic tradition in the Mishnah[1], Rabbi Elazar stated, "All agree [. . .] with regard to the holiday *Shavuot* (Feast of Weeks, or Pentecost) . . . It is the day on which the Torah was given" (Pesachim 68b). This evidence suggests that Pentecost also served as the anniversary of the day that Moses gave the law of the Ten Commandments to Israel (ref. Exodus 20).

Pentecost served great importance to Judaism as one of three annual feasts when Jews returned from their distinct countries to celebrate in Jerusalem. Therefore, it came at the perfect moment for the arrival of the Holy Spirit because, "there were staying in Jerusalem God-fearing Jews from every nation under heaven" (v. 5).

> When the day of Pentecost came, they were all together in one place. Suddenly a sound like the blowing of a violent wind came from heaven and filled the whole house where they were sitting. They saw what seemed to be tongues of fire that separated and came to rest on each of them. All of them were filled with the Holy Spirit and

---

1. The Mishnah is the first written edition of the oral traditions that was called the Oral Torah.

began to speak in other tongues as the Spirit enabled them (vv. 1-4).

The Pentecostal experience did not merely serve as a miracle, but it also brought an explicit connection to the Old Testament. First of all, Moses desired "that all the Lord's people were prophets and that the Lord would put his Spirit on them!" (Numbers 11:29). Secondly, the prophet Joel prophesied that this would happen one day (Joel 2:28-32). Finally, Peter declared that the Pentecost event fulfilled that prophecy (Acts 2:16-21). However, the first filling of the Holy Spirit under the new covenant continued the biblical pattern of prophecy, but this time it took place in the form of tongues.

Peter's Declaration (Acts 4)

With the move of the Holy Spirit, the Church began to grow rapidly, "many who heard the message believed; so the number of men who believed grew to about five thousand" (v. 4). This event greatly impacted the Jewish leadership so "they had Peter and John brought before them and began to question them: 'By what power or what name did you do this?'" (v. 7). The Holy Spirit filled Peter as he boldly addressed the Jewish leaders. Peter's response demonstrated the continuation of the filling of the Holy Spirit, something that now came on a continual basis and not in isolated events as in the Old Testament (vv. 8-12).

The Samaritan Baptism (Acts 8)

Following the outline in Acts 1:8, Luke wrote about the baptism in the Holy Spirit in the region of Judea and Samaria. In chapter 8 (vv. 4-13), Philip went to Samaria to proclaim Christ and did miraculous signs, exercised evil spirits, and healed the people. Many believed the Word of God, including a sorcerer named Simon.

The apostles Peter and John found out about the revival in Samaria and "When they arrived, they prayed for them that they might receive the Holy Spirit" (v. 15). This passage develops two interesting points: (1) Luke demonstrates that the Samaritans are believers, but had not yet received the baptism in the Holy Spirit; and (2) Peter and John stress that these Samaritans receive the baptism in the Holy Spirit. So, Luke taught that the baptism in the Holy Spirit is a subsequent experience to salvation and that the apostles expected that all believers were baptized in the Spirit.

"Then Peter and John placed their hands on them, and they received the Holy Spirit" (v. 17). Here Luke did not openly discuss what happened when the Samaritans received the Holy Spirit, but something incredible did happen. "When Simon (the sorcerer) saw that the Spirit was given at the laying on of the apostles' hands, he offered them money" (v. 18). So, what did Simon see? Many theories and ideas exist about what happened in that account, but biblically, we need to remember that up to this moment in the Bible, the pattern always followed a prophetic expression. There-fore, we should expect nothing less, and Luke gave us a clue as to what happened when he cited Peter's response to Simon. "Peter answered: 'May your money perish with you, because you thought you could buy *the* gift of God with money!'" (v. 20).

Grammatically, the word "the" is the definite article. In Eng-lish, we use it to express something specific. For example, if you say, "I want *a* pencil," it means that you want any pencil because you do not specify which pencil. However, if you say, "I want *the* pencil," it grammatically means that you have the specific pencil in mind. The concept of the definite article is even stronger in the Greek of this passage. In first century Greek, when someone used the definite article, it meant that they had just one thing in mind. So, when Peter said, "*the* gift of God", he understood that there was just one specific gift. Two chapters later in Acts 10 Peter explains what *the* gift was that Simon the sorcerer saw.

Saul's Baptism (Acts 9)

In Acts 9 Luke discusses the move of the Holy Spirit in the re-gion of Judea with Saul persecuting the Christians all the way to

Damascus. However, "As he neared Damascus on his journey, suddenly a light from heaven flashed around him. He fell to the ground and heard a voice say to him, 'Saul, Saul, why do you persecute me?' 'Who are you, Lord?' Saul asked. 'I am Jesus, whom you are persecuting,' he replied" (vv. 3-5).

Saul's experience with Jesus temporarily blinded him, yet he followed the Lord's instructions to go to the house of Ananias. There, Saul converted to Christianity and began to serve Christ. "Then Ananias went to the house and entered it. Placing his hands on Saul, he said, 'Brother Saul, the Lord—Jesus, who appeared to you on the road as you were coming here—has sent me so that you may see again and be filled with the Holy Spirit' (v. 17). The following verse states that something like scales fell off Saul's eyes and he was baptized. However, Luke did not state that he spoke in tongues, but some believe that he did so that Ananias had the evidence that he really was saved. In all honestly, no one really knows, but later Paul did speak in tongues when he wrote to the church in Corinth, "I thank God that I speak in tongues more than all of you" (1 Corinthians 14:18).

Gentiles Baptized at Cornelius' House (Acts 10)

From Saul in Judea, Luke transitioned to the last part of his outline—to the ends of the earth with the Gentiles. In chapter 10, Luke introduced a Roman centurion, a man that made his riches doing horrible things to achieve a high rank, and his own house. The Jews hated the Romans for occupying their land and oppressing their people. They saw them as an unscrupulous, immoral, and filthy people.

Therefore, Luke focused on a vision that Peter had of impure things. In the vision Peter didn't want to touch or eat any of them, but God told him, "Do not call anything impure that God has made clean" (v. 15). This vision prepared Peter to go to the house of an impure Roman centurion, Cornelius. Peter went to his house accompanied by Jewish chaperones, and realized that like his vision, God had purified this Roman. So, Peter preached to him. . .

> While Peter was still speaking these words, the Holy Spirit came on all who heard the message. The circumcised believers who had come with Peter were astonished that *the* gift of the Holy Spirit had been poured out even on Gentiles. For they heard them speaking in tongues and praising God (vv. 44-46).

For a second time, Peter uses the term, "*the* gift", but this time he clarified it as speaking in tongues. Here the term, "*the* gift" implies that Peter sees just one specific gift linked to the baptism in the Holy Spirit.

Peter Defends His Actions (Acts 11)

Acts 11 records Peter's defense of his actions with Cornelius to the apostles and the Church. They would not have understood why Peter went to the house of a dirty Roman. So Peter defended himself and intentionally reminded them what happened when they were filled with the Holy Spirit and spoke in tongues (Acts 2:4). Peter also connected this experience to what happened with the Romans saying, . . .

> As I began to speak, the Holy Spirit came on them as he had come on us at the beginning. Then I remembered what the Lord had said: 'John baptized with water, but you will be baptized with the Holy Spirit.' So if God gave them the same gift he gave us who believed in the Lord Jesus Christ, who was I to think that I could stand in God's way?" (vv. 15-17).

For the third time, Peter used the definite article, "*the* gift" to connect the filling of the Holy Spirit with just one gift of evidence. The first time in Acts 8:20 he mentioned that there is an evidential gift. The second time in 10:45 Peter clarified that, *the* gift is tongues. Then in 11:17, he connected *the* gift of tongues to the Day of Pentecost experience that he and the other disciples experienced in 2:4. So Luke intentionally weaves these events into his narrative to show Theophilus that the evidence of the filling of the Holy Spirit comes in the form of speaking in tongues.

Paul's Declaration (Acts 13)

In this chapter Luke recorded that Saul (now Paul) went with his mentor, Barnabas and some other brothers, from Antioch on their first missionary journey. Upon arriving on the island of Cyprus they went to the city of Paphos. There they encountered a sorcerer and "Paul, filled with the Holy Spirit, looked straight at Elymas (the sorcerer) and said, 'You are a child of the devil and an enemy of everything that is right! You are full of all kinds of deceit and trickery. . .'" (vv. 9-10a).

Luke never mentioned that Paul spoke in tongues in chapter 9 when he received the filling of the Holy Spirit. Yet it is clear here that three years later, Paul did have the gift of prophecy and continued to move in the Holy Spirit. In 1 Corinthians 14:18, Paul revealed that he did indeed speak in tongues.

The Jerusalem Council (Acts 15)

In Acts 15, Luke included the minutes of the Jerusalem Council as a scene change in his narrative. Until this moment, his record traced the movement of the Holy Spirit according Jesus' outline in the first chapter—Jerusalem, then Judea and Samaria, and then to the ends of the earth. Luke demonstrated that process in his first 14 chapters, but in chapter 15 he expressed a problem that this growth caused.

Up to this moment in early Church history, thousands of Jews and Gentiles had converted. However, some of the Jewish Christians wanted to impose the law of Moses on the Gentile Christians demanding that, "Unless you are circumcised, according to the custom taught by Moses, you cannot be saved" (v. 1b). That imposition caused a great divide in the early church, so the apostles and other key leaders called for a meeting in Jerusalem to deal with the problem.

Luke mentioned that Paul and Barnabas came to the Jerusalem Council (v. 2). Peter (v. 7), and James (v. 13) also came. These key church leaders referred to the miracles that God had done among them. Peter again, connected their experience on the Day of Pentecost with what was happening to the Gentiles saying, "God, who knows the heart, showed that he accepted them by giving the Holy Spirit to them, just as he did to us. He did not discriminate between us and them, for he purified their hearts by faith" (vv. 8-9). Peter referred to the gift of tongues when he said *"just as he did to us"*, he also referred to the event with Cornelius and his household of dirty Romans when he said, *"he purified their hearts"*.

James was able to show the group that the Gentiles truly converted (v. 19). However, in this chapter Luke revealed the initial evidence that Paul, Barnabas, Peter, James, and the other apostles and church elders looked for to know that someone had received the baptism in the Holy Spirit. These early church leaders looked for the same gift that they had received when they were baptized on the Day of Pentecost—speaking in other tongues.

Luke developed the series in Acts to this moment, selecting specific narratives to show Theophilus that God established a biblical pattern for the filling of the Holy Spirit. Luke's series points in the direction of one gift of evidence in the New Testament—speaking in tongues. The filling of the Holy Spirit exists to empower the advancement of the Great Commission.

The Ephesian Baptism (Acts 19)

Luke recorded his last account of the filling of the Holy Spirit on Paul's third missionary journey. There, Paul decided to pass through Ephesus to see the development of the church he had planted. When he arrived, Paul met twelve disciples and began to talk with them.

> (He) asked them, "Did you receive the Holy Spirit *when* you believed?" They answered, "No, we have not even heard that there is a Holy Spirit." So Paul asked, "Then what baptism did you receive?" John's baptism," they replied. Paul said, "John's baptism was a baptism of

repentance. He told the people to believe in the one coming after him, that is, in Jesus (vv. 2-4).

In English, many versions translate verse 2 as, "*when* you believed". However, the King James Version translated this phrase, "*since* you believed". The difference between the words *when* and *since* may seem insignificant, but it has caused a heated debate among Christians. Theologians argue over the translation because one means that Christians receive the Holy Spirit at the moment they believe (when), while the other means that they receive the Holy Spirit after they believe (since).[2]

Paul demonstrated in verse 2 that someone can receive the baptism in the Holy Spirit in the moment that they believe or after. This passage also emphasizes that a believer should be baptized in the Holy Spirit. Luke directly highlighted Paul's concern, when he found out that these men were followers of Jesus. He was concerned for them to receive the baptism in the Holy Spirit. Paul did not worry about any other experience; therefore, upon Paul's arrival at Ephesus, he immediately prayed that they might receive the baptism in the Holy Spirit, and "when Paul placed his hands on them, the Holy Spirit came on them, and they spoke in tongues and prophesied" (v. 6).

Both Luke and Paul knew that the Ephesian disciples received the baptism in the Holy Spirit because they spoke in other tongues. As far as the apostles and the other early church leaders were concerned, this experience served as the evidence for them to know that the baptism experience had occurred—in connection with the rest of the Bible with the events of the filling of the Holy Spirit and the prophetic expression.

---

2. Greek scholar, J.M. Everts, responds to the dichotomy over the translation of Acts 19:2 stating, "So which interpretation is right? It is essential to recognize that both are based on legitimate understanding of the use of the aorist adverbial participle in Koine Greek. Even in context, it is virtually impossible to prefer one over the other, and theological concerns usually determine which interpretation is chosen. So both interpretations can be considered correct understandings of Paul's question in Acts 19:2 (Everts 2009, 257).

Summary

Luke wrote both of his books (Luke and Acts) to one single person—Theophilus (Luke 1:1-4; Acts 1:1-3). Luke did not write a general history of the life of Christ and the early Church. So, if Luke did not intend to write a general history, what did he intend? We find the answer in the content of his book. For Luke, the Holy Spirit was the constant throughout both of his books.

Luke served as a kind of bridge between the testaments. In his gospel, Luke showed the Old Testament biblical pattern with the filling of the Spirit and its expression in general prophecy. However, in the book of Acts, Luke showed that things slightly changed after the crucifixion. After the cross, when someone experienced the filling of the Holy Spirit, the initial expression still came as prophecy, but now in a more specific form—tongues. This change happened because Christ began a new covenant when he fulfilled the law when he died on the cross. Therefore, Luke demonstrated normative Christianity to Theophilus, and what he should expect.

Chapter 5

What Did Paul Say?

Introduction

THE EVENTS OF ACTS show us that the initial evidence of the baptism in the Holy Spirit comes in the form of the gift of tongues. Luke also implied that this experience is normative or expected for believers. However, it appears that Paul's writings teach the baptism in the Holy Spirit as something that happens the moment someone believes. Paul also seemed to teach about the gift of tongues as something optional rather than normative for the believer. Therefore, this chapter deals with this apparent conflict, which in reality is no conflict at all.[1]

After giving a list of distinct gifts of the Spirit, Paul asked a sarcastic question, "Do all speak in tongues?" (1 Corinthians 12:30b). The context of this passage refers to the many parts of the body of Christ, where different members have different gifts. So, if all believers are not supposed to speak in tongues, then it appears that Luke and Paul contradicted each other. Then who's right, Paul,

1. "The gift of the Spirit in Luke's perspective differs from Paul's perspective (Romans 8:9). For Luke, the gift of the Spirit has a vocational purpose and equips the disciples for service. Thus, it is devoid of any soteriological connotations (meaning it is not a part of salvation). . . It does not mean that it is God's giving of the Spirit which makes a man a Christian. In Acts the Spirit is given to those who are already Christians, that is, to disciples (19:1) and believers (8:12, 19:2)" (Stronstad 1984, 64).

or Luke? The answer is both, because they actually don't contradict each other.

Paul dedicated three chapters of 1 Corinthian (12-14), to discuss spiritual gifts, and the majority of that those chapters deal with tongues. The gift of tongues created as much controversy in the early Church then as it does today. However, just because something is difficult to understand, because it's supernatural, or controversial does not mean we can ignore it. So what did Paul's say about tongues?

Paul and His Baptism Experience
(Acts 9 & 1 Corinthians 14)

First of all, the Holy Spirit filled Paul when Ananias laid hands on him and prayed for him (Acts 9:17). Luke's record does not mention that Paul spoke in tongues, yet Paul himself admitted that he spoke in tongues more than any of the Corinthian believers (1 Corinthians 14:18).

Paul in the Jerusalem Council (Acts 15)

At the Jerusalem Council (Acts 15) Paul, along with Barnabas, Peter, and James noted that the Gentiles shared the same prophetic experience as the day of Pentecost when the disciples received the baptism in the Holy Spirit and spoke in tongues. Therefore, they did not worry about the issue of circumcision since it was obvious that the Holy Spirit had already given his approval of them when they believed. Tongues served as the prophetic sign that Paul and the other apostles looked for to confirm the Holy Spirit baptism.

Paul with the Ephesian Disciples (Acts 19)

At the end of Paul's third missionary journey, he stopped at Ephesus on the way back to Jerusalem. There he found a group of disciples. This group had already accepted Christ, but had not received the

Holy Spirit yet. Paul didn't worry that each of these twelve disciples received a different spiritual gift. However, Paul did concern himself that they receive the baptism in the Holy Spirit. So he prayed and, "when Paul placed his hands on them, the Holy Spirit came on them, and they spoke in tongues and prophesied" (v. 6).

Paul and the Intersession of the Holy Spirit (Romans 8)

When Paul wrote to the believers in Rome, he explained the common Christian experience in prayer. ". . . the Spirit helps us in our weakness. We do not know what we ought to pray for, but the Spirit himself intercedes for us with groans that words cannot express" (v. 26). When Paul wrote that the Spirit "intercedes" he used a compound word meaning "to intercede over", or "to speak on behalf", meaning it happens on a regular and/or continual basis.[2] Therefore according to Paul, when we don't know what to pray, we should regularly and continually allow the Spirit to prophetically intercede for us.

Paul, Did Tongues Cease? (1 Corinthians 13)

After Paul's discourse on love in 1 Corinthians (13), he transitioned to discuss the last days. He stated, "Love never fails. But where there are prophecies, they will cease; where there are tongues, they will be stilled; where there is knowledge, it will pass away. For we know in part and we prophesy in part, but when perfection comes, the imperfect disappears" (vv. 8-10).

Some people have told me that these verses mean that Paul taught that tongues would cease after the death of the apostles and that they existed only for the foundation of the early church since the New Testament didn't exist yet. Unfortunately, this view creates several problems, first of all, it has no biblical support. The Bible never states that tongues or prophecy existed for the foundation of the Church. Secondly, this view takes Paul's words out of context.

---

2. Paul's term, *huperentugchanei* is in the continuous aspect of Koiné Greek.

Paul discussed the last days, "when perfection comes". Even if Paul held this cessationist theory, it would mean that knowledge would also have passed away, which is ridiculous. Prophecy is communication inspired by God, but when perfection comes in the New Jerusalem, we will find ourselves face-to-face with God and not need prophecy because he will communicate directly with us. The prophet Joel and the apostle Peter explained that during the last days; until perfection comes, tongues and prophecy would continue (Joel 2:28-32; Acts 2:16-21). Therefore, Paul did not contradict Luke, he just expressed the limit of when tongues and prophecy will cease.

Paul and Tongues in Corporate Worship (1 Corinthians 14)

In the following chapter of 1 Corinthians, Paul again transitioned from his discourse on love to discuss charismatic gifts. He commanded, "*Follow* the way of love and *eagerly desire* gifts of the Spirit, especially prophecy" (v. 1). Paul also expressed his desire, "I would like every one of you to speak in tongues. . ." (v. 5b). He used the rest of this chapter to explain how to correctly use the gifts of tongues, prophecy, and the interpretation of tongues in corporate worship. In his letter, Paul dealt with the problem of chaos and abuse of the prophetic gifts in the Corinthian church. Therefore, he didn't conflict with Luke's explanations of tongues, he just clarified its use.

Paul and Spiritual Battle (Ephesians 6)

Paul ends his letter to the Ephesian church about spiritual battle encouraging them, ". . . pray in the Spirit on all occasions with all kinds of prayer and requests. . ." (Ephesians 6:18a). Paul commanded the Ephesians to pray in the Spirit as part of their spiritual disciplines to help them as they enter into spiritual battle.

Summary

Did Paul contradict Luke's theology of tongues as a normative Christian experience? From what we have read, it appears to be a big, "NO". Paul himself spoke in tongues on a regular basis. He agreed with Peter at the Jerusalem Council that it was the sign of the Holy Spirit baptism. Paul expected tongues as a normative Christian experience for the Ephesian disciples, for the Roman believers, and for the whole Ephesian church. Therefore, the question remains, "Why did Paul sarcastically ask, 'Do all speak in tongues?'" Well, he simply stated that not all do, but an exegetical analysis of his teaching would equally suggest that all should seek to do so in regard to this particular spiritual gift.

Conclusions

The New Testament record continued the Old Testament biblical pattern. In the Old Testament after the Holy Spirit filled someone, their initial response was general prophecy. In the New Testament, after the Holy Spirit filled someone, their initial response was also prophecy, but under the new covenant it came in a more specific form, through the gift of tongues. Peter called this gift, *"the gift"* of the Holy Spirit. Therefore he, and the other apostles and early church elders looked for that specific gift as evidence to confirm the filling of the Holy Spirit. Paul went a step further to pray for people to makes sure they had received the baptism. Paul encouraged people to seek this gift and he desired them to have it.

According to the New Testament, the gift of tongues had several purposes: (1) for the Spirit to intercede for believers; (2) to function together with the gift of interpretation for unbelievers; and (3) as evidence of the baptism in the Holy Spirit. Our panoramic journey through the New Testament reveals that every believer should seek the baptism in the Holy Spirit to fulfill our part in the Great Commission, something impossible without God's help. We know we have received this empowerment from the same biblical pattern, prophetic expression. Since we are a people under the new covenant, we can expect that evidence to come in the form of tongues. However, this does not mean we should seek the gift, but rather the Giver and leave the rest up to him.

Some people may ask, "So if we're all supposed to speak in tongues when we're baptized in the Holy Spirit, then why hasn't anyone spoken in tongues until the twentieth century?" Well, that kind of a question comes from a lack of knowledge of Church history. Prophecy and even tongues actually did continue. So let's explore it in the next section.

Part IV

The Filling of the Holy Spirit in Church History

SOME EVANGELICAL MOVEMENTS OPPOSE a Pentecostal perspective to the filling of the Holy Spirit and its connection to prophetic speech with the gift of tongues in Church history. They assume that the Pentecostal understanding of tongues does not match the biblical description of the gift, or that the historical accounts are different than classical Pentecostalism (MacArthur 1992, 270-279). However, this argument misunderstands the Pentecostal perspective of tongues.

Biblically the use of tongues varied in several ways. I noted in the previous chapters that according to the apostles, the gift of tongues is *the* gift of the Holy Spirit and *the* initial sign of the Holy Spirit's baptism. Tongues can also exist as a prayer language that allows the Holy Spirit to intercede for the believer with unknown sounds for personal edification (Romans 8:26). Tongues can come in the form of a known human language (Acts 2:4), or an unknown angelic language (1 Corinthians 13:1). Tongues also have a purpose in corporate worship, for edification of the body of Christ (1 Corinthians 14:1-25). However, the Holy Spirit gives this gift, it is not something that people learn or acquire (1 Corinthians 12:11). So we can't think of tongues in such a narrow way that makes the gift impossible or too mystical for anyone to legitimately experience after the early church period.

The historical accounts of this section refer to the Church after the time of the apostles in the New Testament. During these centuries, different groups developed odd and even incorrect doctrines and practices. The purpose of this section and book goes beyond the argument of those theological issues. Rather I focus on the fact that Church history displays the continual use of the gift of tongues, and that prophecy continued. Church history also shows that Christians even expected tongues in connection with the filling of the Holy Spirit. In short, the prophetic gift of tongues and the baptism in the Holy Spirit did not stop after the time of the apostles. An exhaustive account of the filling of the Holy Spirit throughout Church history is far beyond the scope of this book; however, this section does take us on a journey through key historical examples of the biblical pattern of this gift throughout the centuries.

Chapter 6

The Emerging Church

(1st—3rd Centuries)

Introduction

AFTER THE DEATH OF the apostles in the first century, their disciples carried the Church as it emerged under continued Roman oppression, battling many types of heresies. This period of Church history saw the beginnings of a governmental structure for the Church, but filled with much controversy. One of the greatest struggles for the emerging church dealt with the fact that virtually no city had all of the writings of the New Testament. The Gospels, Acts, Epistles, and Revelation were scattered across the Roman Empire and Africa. As a result, people developed doctrines and theologies based on partial understandings of Scripture. Due to these odd doctrines many of the writings and individuals in this chapter have received sharp criticism and scrutiny by their peers and Church historians. However, we must remember that they did their best to serve God with the limited knowledge that they had at the time.

Regardless of the challenges that faced the emerging church, one factor seems to remain constant—the prophetic movement of the Holy Spirit. Although the men and women of the first three centuries of the Church may have developed odd doctrines, the writings they left us demonstrate that the filling of the Holy Spirit and prophecy were a normal part of the Church. This chapter briefly shows evidence of the continuation of the filling of the Spirit and prophetic gifts during this era of Church history.

The Didache (1st Century)

In 1873 Philotheos Bryennius, an Eastern Orthodox Bishop, discovered the *Didache*, a book written in Syria from the first century, and forgotten in the Jerusalem Monastery in Constantinople. *Didache* means "teaching" in Greek, and is the short name for the book's full title, *The Teaching of the Twelve Apostles*. The text specifically teaches about three positions of leadership: (1) Apostles, (2) Teachers or Catechists, and (3) Prophets, or men who "speak in ecstasy", meaning prophecy or an unknown language (Schaff 2014). No one seems to know if any of the twelve apostles actually wrote the *Didache*, but whoever the author, he lived as a contemporary to their lives and ministries. The *Didache* also continued with frequent use in Egypt until the fourth century.

The *Didache* refers to prophecy with a high regard for the prophet who speaks, "Do not test or examine any prophet who is speaking in a spirit, for every sin shall be forgiven, but this sin shall not be forgiven" (Did. 11:7) However, the book does not encourage blind acceptance, reminding the reader that "not everyone who speaks in a spirit is a prophet, except he have the behaviour of the Lord. From his behaviour, then, the false prophet and the true prophet shall be known" (Did. 11:8). The *Didache* expected leaders to fulfill Paul's requirements in his letters to Timothy (3:1-11) and Titus (1:6-9), that they be filled with the Spirit, and prophesy. These requirements reflect the church leaders' view in the Jerusalem Council (Acts 15), that the evidence of the filling of the Holy Spirit came in a prophetic form. The *Didache* states, ...

> Appoint therefore for yourselves bishops and deacons worthy of the Lord, meek men, and not lovers of money, and truthful and approved, for they also minister to you the ministry of the prophets and teachers. Therefore, do

not despise them, for they are your honourable men together with the prophets and teachers (Did. 15:1-2).

This important piece of Church history demonstrates that the
prophetic gifts continued beyond the life of the apostles for centuries; thus, giving evidence of the continuation the biblical pattern
of the filling of the Holy Spirit and prophetic utterance.

Pope Clement of Rome (1st Century)

According to Catholic tradition, Clement served as the third bishop of Rome. In his letter to the Corinthians, Clement reinforced
Paul's letter to the same church using the metaphor of the Church
as the body of Christ, he also explained how to use spiritual gifts
correctly (1 Clem. 37:5-38). Although Clement referred to himself
with a prideful attitude, his teaching demonstrates the fact that
church leadership expected of all spiritual gifts, including tongues
(Clement of Rome 1961, 39, 48-49, 114). Clement's historical writings validate that the prophetic gifts actively continued during his
leadership.

Ignatius, Bishop of Antioch (2nd Century)

Ignatius wrote at least seven letters at the beginning of the second
century before he was martyred in Rome in A.D. 117. Though he
did not consider himself a prophet, much of his ministry revealed
that he did have the gift of prophecy. Moreover, his own writings
show that all of the spiritual gifts actively continued in the Church
during his life. In his letter of encouragement to Polycarp, Bishop
of Smyrna, he wrote, "ask for invisible things so that they may
be made manifest to you in order that you may lack nothing and
abound with all spiritual gifts" (Ignatius 1969, 148).

Shepherd of Hermas (2nd Century)

The author of *The Shepherd of Hermas* wrote sometime in the second century and dealt with prophetic problems from his era, including tongues. The book ends with an encouragement to listen to the one who "full of the Spirit, speaks prophetic words" (Hermans 1956, 43-45). In the text, Hermas experienced visions, and on two occasions, he was told to publish them (Aleph 46:2; 114:1-4). Though this document includes some peculiar teachings and accounts, the fact remains that the prophetic gifts are active during this point in history.

Justin Martyr (2nd Century)

Justin served as an early Christian philosopher who defended the faith until his martyr in the middle of the second century. In Justin's *Dialogue with Trypho*, he provided a unique contribution to Church history. "As we have seen, and will see, a number of these (church fathers) either experienced the gifts or made reference to them. However, Justin actually teaches about them" (Kydd 1984, 26). In the same book he stated that individuals "are also receiving gifts" (Scaff 2014, Loc. 8,186). Martyr also wrote in the same document, "For the prophetical gifts remain with us, even to the present time" (Scaff 2014, Loc. 9,122). These writings clearly show that prophetic gifts were active and common in the second century Church.

Irenaeus, Archbishop of Lyon (2nd Century)

A disciple of the Bishop Polycarp in Smyrna, Irenaeus moved from Asia Minor to Gaul, (modern day France) to serve as the Bishop of the city of Lyon. During his tenure as Bishop, many in his church had received the baptism in the Holy Spirit and spoke in tongues.

> As also we hear that many brethren in the Church possess prophetic gifts, and speak, through the Spirit, with

all kinds of tongues, and bring to light the secret things of men for their good, and declare the mysteries of God (Schaff 2014, Loc. 448,752).

Among many other accounts, Irenaeus recorded that tongues and prophecy were common and continual in his congregation. Irenaeus also intentionally linked the gift of tongues to the filling of the Holy Spirit. This connection referred directly to Luke's perspective in Acts.

Montanus (2nd Century)

Montanus was a pagan priest who lived in Phrygia (modern day southern Turkey). When Montanus converted to Christianity, "he was carried away in spirit, and wrought up into a certain kind of frenzy and irregular ecstasy, raving, and speaking, and uttering strange things, and proclaiming what was contrary to the institutions that had prevailed in the church. . ." (Eusebius 1998, 171-173). This prophetic record closely paralleled the case of Cornelius and his household who spoke in tongues when they converted to Christianity (Acts 10:44-46) (Eusebius 1961, 231).

Montanus' teachings rose to popularity through the eighth century and many other church fathers followed Montanism Christianity. Those followers also often expressed prophetic utterances and some in the form of tongues. Although Montanism created much controversy over the ages, it gives us a glimpse into a range of centuries where the filling of the Spirit continued to function in connection with the gift of tongues.

Origen (2nd Century)

Origen served as a teacher and the head at the Catechetical School in Alexandria, Egypt. Historians consider him one of the greatest scholars of the ancient church. In his work *Against Celsus*, Origen stated, ". . . this diviner method is called by the apostle the 'manifestation of the Spirit and of power': of 'the Spirit.' On account of the prophecies. . ." (Scaff 2014, Loc. 77,739). This meant that "Those living a Christian life guided by the Spirit expel evil spirits, perform many cures, and foresee certain events. They receive gifts of language, wisdom, and knowledge" (Burgess 2011, 42). Therefore, Origen likely taught future church leaders in Egypt the gift of tongues accompanied the filling of the Holy Spirit.

Tertullian of Carthage (3rd Century)

Tertullian lived as a priest and early Christian author who fiercely battled Gnosticism. He also followed Montanism teachings. In his study of Montanism, Tertullian wrote in his *Treatise Against Praxeas*, about two prophetesses who served as disciples of Montanus and "prophesied in ecstasy", or speaking in tongues (Schaff 2014, 61,753).

Due to Tertullian's argumentative nature, and the controversies that surrounded Montanism, many church leaders considered his writings controversial. However, the fact remains that prophecy and tongues were common and even expected in Carthage during his life in the third century.

Cyprian, Archbishop of Carthage (3rd Century)

In the middle of the third century Cyprian, the Archbishop of Carthage, reported that prophesy connected to the filling of the Spirit. He wrote, "In addition to visions in the night, during the day also among us the innocent age of childhood is filled with the Holy Spirit. It sees with its eyes in ecstasy, it hears, and it speaks those things of which the Lord thinks it is worthwhile to warn and to instruct us" (Kydd translation 1984, 74). In Cyprian's region of North Africa, the connection between the filling of the Holy Spirit, and the evidence of prophetic expression existed as a normal occurrence.

Novation (3rd Century)

Novation served as a church elder in Rome in the mid third century and attempted to become bishop. However, after the church leadership overlooked him, he focused on writing. In one of his works, *Concerning the Trinity*, he highlighted the continuation of the spiritual gifts stating, . . :

> This is He who places prophets in the Church, instructs teachers, directs tongues, gives powers and healings, does wonderful works, offers discrimination of spirits, affords powers of government, suggests counsels, and orders and arranges whatever other gifts there are of charismata; and thus make the Lord's Church everywhere, and in all, perfected and completed (Scaff 2014, Loc. 108, 430).

Novation did not coincidentally write a parallel to Paul's list of diverse spiritual gifts (1 Corinthians 12:1-11). This text serves as direct evidence that all spiritual gifts functioned throughout the third century in Rome.

Conclusion

As the early church grew and emerged in the Roman world, the Romans began to recognize Christianity as its own religion rather than a Jewish sect. However, this heightened attention and broad growth only increased persecution from the Romans. The continual growth of the faith and limited access to all of the New Testament writings also created an environment where isolated groups developed unorthodox doctrines. However, regardless of the challenges the Church faced during this period, the writers I mention in this chapter demonstrated a constant; the Holy Spirit continued to fill individuals and prophetically speak through them.

Chapter 7

The Established Church
(4th—9th Centuries)

Introduction

DURING FIRST THREE CENTURIES, Christianity continued to spread throughout the Roman Empire, yet the Roman leadership limited its growth through their ever growing persecution. The Church knew Emperor Diocletian (A.D. 244-311) as an aggressive persecutor of Christians. However, everything began to change at the close of the third century; Diocletian had Christians in his household, including his wife and daughter. Yet, he still "intensified the persecution until A.D. 311 when, as he was dying, he issued his edict of toleration" (Hicks 1992, 264). This new law stopped state approved persecution against the Christians and allowed for a new age of growth and establishment for the Church.

Soon after the Romans lifted their sanctions against Christianity, a new emperor, Constantine I, came to power. As the first openly Christian emperor, Constantine organized the first major council of Christian bishops to come to agreement on church doctrine. This council, held in Nicaea, Asia Minor produced the Nicene Creed in A.D. 325 which the Church later used as the basis for standard Christian doctrine today. The creed states: . . .

> We believe in one God, the Father Almighty, Maker of all things visible and invisible. And in one Lord Jesus Christ, the Son of God, begotten of the Father [the only-begotten; that is, of the essence of the Father, God of God,] Light of Light, very God of very God, begotten, not made, being of one substance with the Father; By whom all things were made [both in heaven and on earth]; Who for us men, and for our salvation, came down and was incarnate and was made man; He suffered, and the third day he rose again, ascended into heaven; From thence he shall come to judge the quick and the dead. And in the Holy Ghost. [But those who say: 'There was a time when he was not;' and 'He was not before he was made;' or 'He is of another substance' or 'essence,' or 'The Son of God is created,' or 'changeable,' or 'alterable'— they are condemned by the holy catholic and apostolic Church.] (Schaff 1877, 27).

From this point forward the Church developed a more united organization with an extensive network, and grew to become the official religion of the Roman Empire. The Church centralized its leadership under to the archbishop in Rome, the capital and most influential location. That bishop became known as the father (or in Latin, "Papa") of the universal (or Catholic) Church. Today we call that man the Pope. Unfortunately, the Pope's leadership grew with governmental support until the Church's power and influence reached unimaginable levels. During these centuries the Roman Catholic Church developed as it we know it today. Regardless of the drastic changes that occurred during this period, this chapter explores how the move of the Holy Spirit continued the biblical patterns set in the previous centuries.

Saint Antony of the Desert (4th Century)

Born to a relatively wealthy Christian family in Egypt, Antony's parents died shortly after he turned eighteen. Due to his age, Antony inherited everything. However, history records that he was impacted by Jesus' words to the rich young man in Matthew 19:21,

"If you want to be perfect, go, sell your possessions and give to the poor, and you will have treasure in heaven. Then come, follow me." Antony sold nearly everything and adopted an ascetic lifestyle living as a recluse near the base of a mountain. Church history also considers Antony as the father of monasticism because his lifestyle drew many to follow his example living as monks. Athanasius, Bishop of Alexandria, wrote a history of the life of Antony. In his work he included many miracles and fillings of the Holy Spirit which resulted in prophetic expressions (Meyer 1950).

Saint Macarius of Egypt (4th Century)

Several decades after Antony popularized the monastic lifestyle, Macarius also from Egypt and decided to live in a monastic group in the Scetis Desert (today known as the Wadi El Natrun). Macarius gained a great deal of fame from being "in a state of continual ecstasy [and] was known for exercising gifts of healing and forecasting the future" (Burgess 2011, 53).

When Macarius wrote his *Great Letter: An Allegorical Interpretation of Things under Done under the Law*, he echoed the Apostle Paul's theology of circumcision of the heart versus the flesh (Romans 2:28-29). Macarius wrote, "With them was a baptism sanctifying the flesh, but with us there is a baptism in the Holy Spirit and fire. . . Therefore, the Lord consoles us through the working of the Spirit in our every tribulation to save us and communicate to us all his spiritual and charismatic gifts" (Maloney 1992, 155-156). Although the allegorical interpretations of the early church fathers are incorrect interpretations of Scripture, this account still represents a prophetic connection with the baptism in the Holy Spirit in the fourth century.

Saint Basil of Cappadocia (4th Century)

Basil, along with his brother St. Gregory of Nyssa, and his close friend St. Gregory of Nazianzen were known as the Cappadocian

Fathers. Their influence on Church doctrine set the tone for centuries later. Specifically, Basil's teachings on the Holy Spirit still influence the Eastern Orthodox and Catholic Churches today. As a saint who stands out among others for his significant teachings on the Holy Spirit, the Catholic Church gave Basil the rare title of "Doctor of the Church". Basil's doctrinal contributions clarified that the Holy Spirit was not a force of God, or lesser in importance to the Father or Son, but an equal and separate person in unity with the other members of the Trinity. At the time Basil's teachings revolutionized Church doctrine and still influences Catholic, Orthodox, and Protestant churches today.

Basil emphasized Paul's teaching on the Holy Spirit (ref. 1 Corinthians 12:27-31) stating, "Since no one has the capacity to receive all spiritual gifts, but the grace of the Spirit is given proportionately to the faith of each, when one is living in community with others, the grace privately bestowed on each individual becomes the common possession of the others" (Bray 1999, 121). Even though Basil's doctrine may differ from the premise of this book, that tongues are normative as the sign of the baptism in the Holy Spirit, his historical account supports the notion that tongues were still common and expected in the Church during his lifetime.

Saint Augustine of Hippo (5th Century)

Augustine of Hippo is considered one of the greatest theologians in Church history. Although Augustine came from a Christian home, he struggled with skepticism and sexual addiction. As a young man he moved around from one philosophy to another trying to find answers, as well as moving from one concubine to another. Eventually he came to Milan and was impacted by the Apostle Paul's teaching in Romans, "Let us behave decently, as in the daytime, not in carousing and drunkenness, not in sexual immorality and debauchery, not in dissension and jealousy. Rather, clothe yourselves with the Lord Jesus Christ, and do not think about how to gratify the desires of the flesh" (13:13-14). From that moment, Augustine decided to receive water baptism and dedicate his life to full-time ministry. He eventually returned to Hippo where he ascended as the bishop and served until his death.

Due to Augustine's checkered past, he had the unique ability to integrate philosophies such as Neoplatonism, stoicism, and teachings of Cicero along with the teachings of the Apostle Paul, and the theology of the Nicene Creed. However, this outstanding theologian denied the continuation of the gift of tongues after the apostles of the New Testament. In his *Sixth Homily*, Augustine wrote, . . .

> In the earliest times, "the Holy Ghost fell upon them that believed: and they spake with tongues," which they had not learned, "as the Spirit gave them utterance." These were signs adapted to the time. For there behooved to be that betokening of the Holy Spirit in all tongues, to shew that the Gospel of God was to run through all tongues over the whole earth. That thing was done for a betokening, and it passed away (Schaff 2014, Loc. 317,517).

As Augustine continued his sermon, he began to ask if tongues continued rather than outright deny them. Augustine's own words suggest that he wrestled with this very notion and did not have a definitive answer. At the same time, he actually admitted that tongues were the New Testament sign of the baptism in the Holy Spirit. Therefore, Augustine's own admission, and the historical evidence of his contemporaries demonstrate that the ancient church fathers agreed that tongues served the initial evidence of the baptism in the Holy Spirit.

Saint Isaac, Bishop of Nineveh (7th Century)

Isaac taught that divine knowledge goes beyond the human ability to comprehend, and that man needs the filling of the Holy Spirit to achieve such knowledge. He stated, . . .

> It is in this state, therefore, that the Holy Ghost joins with the things which man prays, some unattainable insights, which it stirs in him in accordance with his aptitude of being moved so that by these insights the emotion of

prayer ceases, the mind is absorbed in ecstasy and the desired object of prayer is forgotten (Wensinck 1923, 34).

The context of Isaac's statement infers a connection between tongues and the move of the Holy Spirit. Yet, even if it didn't he implied an understanding of the continuation of tongues with a connection to the filling of the Holy Spirit.

Armenian Paulicianism (4th—9th Centuries)

The Paulicians formed as a subgroup within the Church during the middle ages. They defied the Church establishment questioning their authority and its traditions of salvation based on sacraments and the worship of Mary or the Saints. In short, this movement had many of the same concerns with the Church as the reformers, such as Martin Luther. As this group rejected much of the Church tradition that had developed over the first millennia, many focused on a return to the authority of the Bible, a doctrine later called *sola scriptura* (Scripture alone).

At the end of the nineteenth century, Frederick Cornwallis Conybeare, a theology professor from Oxford, discovered an ancient text called *They Key of Truth* in a library in Armenia. The teachings of this text reflect the Paulicians who once lived there. Although this text contains some strange teachings, it makes an interesting statement.

> And (Though Holy Spirit) didst make him (Jesus Christ) king and head of beings in heaven and in earth and under the earth; even as St. Paul, filled with thee, declareth. Furthermore, thou didst divide the fiery tongues unto the holy Apostles and unite them unto the one word, and didst make them the Catholic Church of the Son of God the Father. And now with all reverence do we entreat thee that thou come down into these and fill the hearts of the baptized who have now been baptized into Christ Jesus, lest peradventure the unclean spirit approach them that have believed in the only born son of the heavenly Father (Conybeare 1898, 109).

In this passage, the Armenian branch of the Paulician movement teaches that when the Holy Spirit filled the Apostle Paul, and the gift of tongues was poured out as a sign of the baptism in the Holy Spirit on the Apostles, they desired and expected the same experience. This evidence explains the connection of the baptism in the Holy Spirit to the gift of tongues in the ninth century.

Conclusion

Though there may be odd doctrines or allegorical teachings that came from this section of history, this journey reveals people's mindset, desiring a relationship and filling of the Holy Spirit in the same fashion as the New Testament experience. The people of the established church understood that of tongues or prophecy should accompany the baptism in the Holy Spirit just like in the biblical pattern.

Chapter 8

The Medieval Church
(10th—14th Centuries)

Introduction

THE LATTER MIDDLE AGES served as a time of embarrassment for the Church. In the middle of the eleventh century the eastern portion of the Roman Empire officially broke away both politically and religiously, and formed the Eastern Orthodox Church. Several decades later, Pope Urban II initiated the first crusade to take back the Holy Land from Muslim conquest. This offensive initiated centuries of bloodshed in the crusades and resulted in an embarrassing period in the history of the Catholic Church. This dark era of the middle ages was also plagued with high illiteracy, mysticism, and blind legalism to traditions that no longer served their purpose. Due to these challenges, many theological teachings also include odd and erroneous doctrines. However, writings from this era also show a continued dependence on the Holy Spirit and the continuance of the gift of tongues. This chapter focuses on key historical accounts that demonstrate the continuation of this gift despite the grievous political and theological blunders.

Symeon (10th Century)

Symeon lived as a monk from Constantinople, and frequently experienced visions from God. He believed in the continuation of the baptism in the Holy Spirit, but erroneously taught that it was necessary for salvation. Symeon also developed a doctrine that tears were the evidence of the baptism in the Holy Spirit. He wrote, "When these (sins) have been blotted out through tears, the soul finds itself in the comfort of the Spirit of God and is watered by streams of sweetest compunction" (de Cantanzaro 1980, 160).

Although Symeon taught erroneous theology on the Holy Spirit, we must realize that his historical record demonstrates that the people from the tenth century still sought the baptism in the Holy Spirit.

Chartres Cathedral, France (12th Century)

In his book, *Sounds of Wonder: A Popular History of Speaking in Tongues in the Catholic Tradition*, Eddie Ensley gives historical examples from the ninth to the sixteen centuries of revivals that included spontaneous worship and tongues. Many of these revivals in the late middle ages resulted in the construction of cathedrals with thousands of volunteers who also confessed their sins and forgave one another. Of these examples, the construction of the cathedral in Chartres, France in the mid twelfth century stands out. Ensley states, . . .

> One letter by a participant in this revival, Abbot Haimon of St. Pierrsur-Dives in Normandy, vividly describes this revival, and the accuracy of his account is attested by other contemporary sources. Charismatic worship healing services and a greater call to conversion were all part of this revival. . . When the priests encouraged the people to repent and seek mercy, they would break into charismatic prayer (Ensley 1977, 63, 66).

The historical account of the construction of the Chartres cathedral recorded individuals who prayed in tongues, and demonstrated that these individuals did not seek the gift, rather the Holy Spirit poured out his gift on them. Furthermore, the gift of tongues was not the greatest miracle, rather it was the revival, authentic repentance of sin, and forgiveness. Relationships were restored and lives were changed. Until this point of Church history, nearly no charismatic event more closely reflected the Pentecostal experience of the New Testament.

Saint Hildegard of Bingen (12th Century)

Arguably one of the most famous women in Church history, Hildegard of Bingen, served as an abbess of a monastery in Bingen (in modern day Germany) during the middle ages. She claimed to have experienced her call in a similar way to the disciples on the day of Pentecost (Acts 2:4). Her detailed account states, . . .

> It happened that, in the eleven hundred and forty-first year of the Incarnation of the Son of God, Jesus Christ, when I was forty-two years and seven months old, heaven was opened and a fiery light of exceeding brilliance came and permeated my whole brain, and inflamed my whole heart and my whole breast, not like a burning but like a warming flame, as the sun warms anything its rays touch (Hart and Bishop 1990, 59).

Hildegard continued to explain how the Scriptures clearly came to her after to this experience. However, "She is remembered for her unknown language (*Lingua Ignota*) or glossolalia, her "concerts" or singing in the Spirit, her ecstatic visions, resulting prophecies and her numerous miracles (Giles 1852, 317-318). Hildegard's prophetic outpouring draws a parallel to the experience of the New Testament and what the apostles looked for in regard to the baptism in the Holy Spirit. With a humble heart she served all and ministered to both the poor and spoke before popes.

Princess Elizabeth of Hungary (13th Century)

Medieval historian, Matthew of Paris, wrote about St. Hildegard and another notable woman from this period who also possessed "the spirit of prophecy and of knowledge and of tongues." St. Elizabeth of Hungary was a princess of the kingdom. After her husband died, she dedicated her life to ministering to the poor. Similar to Hildegard, Elizabeth's experience gives historical evidence that women during the middle ages also experienced the baptism in the Holy Spirit and its evidence of tongues (Higley 2007).

Saint Francis of Assisi (13th Century)

One of the most famous saints of Church history, Francis founded of the Franciscan Order. He lived humbly, as did many monks during his day, and willingly lived in poverty, along with his followers, as a means to preach to others. People often attribute the famous quote, "Preach the Gospel at all times, and if necessary, use words" to him. However, history does not agree. Such a quote does not appear in any of Francis' writings. In fact, his ministry demonstrated quite the opposite, as a powerful preacher full of the Spirit, who regularly prophesied.

Roughly three decades after Francis' death, the historian, Saint Bonaventure wrote the first biography of Francis in his *Legenda Major*. He wrote, "So fully did he possess the spirit of prophecy, that he foretold things to come, and beheld the secrets of hearts, and knew things absent as if they were present. . ." (Manning 1988, 91). This evidence demonstrates that individuals in the thirteenth century still sought the baptism in the Holy Spirit and that the charismatic gifts of prophecy were still active.

Saint Thomas Aquinas (13th Century)

Aquinas was one of the greatest Church philosophers and theologians. Catholics, Evangelicals, and secular institutions still teach much of his theology and philosophy today, which is why he is often called the "Prince of Scholastics". Although many religion scholars love to study Aquinas' rationalist teachings, we can't overlook the fact that he strongly believed in, and practiced the spiritual gifts, or has he put it, "charismatic graces." In his biography on *The Life of St. Thomas Aquinas*, Bernard Gui, a contemporary of Aquinas, pointed out how the Holy Spirit impacted Aquinas.

> In the last year of his life, happening to be at his sister's castle of San Severino with Reginald, his companion, and several other of the brethren, he was rapt in ecstasy almost continuously for three days. . . Thomas was often affected in this way, but that this trance had lasted longer than any previous one in his experience. It was finally ended by Reginald's tugging violently at his master's cloak (Foster 1959, 44).

Aquinas' ecstatic episodes infer intense moments of prayer and meditation that would include tongues. This reference alludes to Paul's teaching on the intersession of the Holy Spirit with inward groans and sounds that words cannot express (ref. Romans 8:26). So, Aquinas actually based his rationalist teachings on supernatural intersession.

Saint Vincent Ferrier of Valencia (14th Century)

Ferrier lived as a Dominican monk, and served as an itinerate missionary across western Europe toward the end of the fourteenth century. Ferrier's fame came from mass conversions from all walks of life, including Muslims in Spain. Although his ministry included miraculous gifts of healing, he also possessed the gift of tongues (Groce 1950, 3037-3042). His contemporary, and Church historian, Pietro Ranzano, Bishop of Lucera, recorded Ferrier's charismatic ministry in his biography *Vita Vincentii*.

> When St. Vincent Ferrier preached, all foreigners understood him. St. Vincent Ferrier went about preaching. He was accompanied by fifty priests, a large number of Tertiaries of the order of St. Dominic, and a multitude of penitents. The audience of strangers amounted often to

ten thousand, but though the crowd was so enormous, the persons furthest off heard him as distinctly as those near him; and although all nationalities were amongst the hearers, Frenchmen and Italians, Germans and English, Spaniards and Portuguese, all understood every word that was uttered, as if it had been spoken in their own language (Ranzano 1834, 155).

Ferrier's experience demonstrated the continuation of the baptism in the Holy Spirit. This evidence closely paralleled the expression of tongues in the New Testament account of the disciples. Acts (2:4-12) records people from different language groups who heard the disciples speaking of God in their native languages. Ferrier's experience also demonstrated similarities to the Jewish tradition of Moses' voice separating into seventy tongues when he gave the law for the first time (see chapter 2).

Conclusion

Regardless of the embarrassing events that stain the history of the medieval Church, history shows that the Holy Spirit continued to baptize believers, and empower them with his charismatic gifts, including tongues. Similar to the many biblical characters full of flaws, the Holy Spirit used the men and women of the medieval Church in spite of their flaws. Though there are many more historical accounts of the filling of the Holy Spirit during this period of history, the key events in this chapter clearly demonstrate that neither the baptism experience, nor the gift of tongues had ceased.

Chapter 9

The Reformed Church
(15th—18th Centuries)

Introduction

THE REFORMATION MOVEMENT CAME to full bear in 1517. On October 31 of that year the German priest, Martin Luther, nailed his ninety-five theses to the door of the Wittenberg church. He opposed many Catholic teachings and practices. Although Luther was not the first to question these issues, his wide-spread concerns and publications marked a significant change in Christianity forevermore.

Luther never wanted to separate from the Catholic Church, he wanted to reform it. However, Luther's reformation sparked a period of protests against the Church. This Protestant movement caused a rapid exodus of denominations that splintered from Catholicism. This period also saw a return to biblical teaching from the traditions and mysticism of the medieval Church. This return resulted in great revivals throughout Europe and the new American colonies. With revivals such as the Great Awakening and the return to biblical doctrine, we begin to see the gifts of the Holy Spirit occur with greater frequency in the historical record.

Martin Luther (16th Century)

Possibly one of the most famous men in Church history, Martin Luther served as a talented priest. Luther desired to see the Church return to biblical teaching with the Bible as the ultimate authority (*sola scriptura*), and not Church tradition or the Papal office. Although most of Luther's fame came from his spark in the Reformation of the Church, he never intended to ignited the Protestant movement. Luther also had much to say about the Holy Spirit and the gift of tongues.

Martin Luther held a deep sensitivity to the Holy Spirit. He felt that the Spirit called, commissioned, and empowered his ministry with spiritual gifts. In his *Small Catechism* he wrote, "The Holy Spirit has called me through the Gospel, enlightened me with his gifts, and sanctified and preserved me in true faith" (Luther 1959, 345). Luther also taught that the spiritual gifts, including tongues, were available to all believers. On Ascension Day 1523, he preached a sermon on Mark 16:17-18 stating, "We must not suppose that the signs here mentioned by Christ are all signs that believers do (exorcisms, speaking with new tongues). . . but Jesus means: All Christians can and may do the signs" (Luther 1983, 3:189). Luther also desired the filling of the Holy Spirit. In the following year, he composed a hymn where the first stanza reads, . . .

> Come, Holy Ghost, God and Lord!
> Be all Thy graces now outpoured
> On each believer's mind and heart;
> Thy fervent love to them impart.
> Lord, by the brightness of thy light,
> Thou in the faith dost men unite
> Of ev'ry land and ev'ry tongue;
> This to Thy praise, O Lord, our God, be sung.
> Hallelujah! Hallelujah! (Luther 1917, 72).

Luther later developed more of a cessationist point of view, similar to Augustine. In 1535 from his *Lectures on Galatians*, he stated, . . .

[In] the first sending forth of the Holy Spirit; it was necessary in the primitive church, which had to be established
with visible signs on account of the unbelievers, as Paul
testifies. 1 Corinthians 14:22: "Tongues are a sign, not
for believers but for unbelievers." But later on, when the
church had been gathered and confirmed by these signs,
it was not necessary for this visible sending forth of the
Holy Spirit to continue (Luther, 1991, 374).

Although later in life, Luther thought that the gift of tongues
had ceased with the apostles, and that individuals no longer need-
ed the gift for his time, he still sought the baptism in Holy Spirit for
himself and all people.

Thomas Müntzer (16th Century)

Martin Luther may have taught that tongues had ceased in his
later years, but his own disciple, Thomas Müntzer, drastically
disagreed with him. In his letter to Luther, Müntzer wrote, "The
recognition of the divine will, which should fill us with wisdom
through Christ, with a spiritual and infallible understanding, this
knowledge of God is to be possessed by all (as the apostle teaches
the Colossians)" (Müntzer 1988, 56). Müntzer also taught that
"each person must receive the Holy Spirit" (Marius 1999, 406).
In contrast to Luther, he understood that the "Holy Spirit gives
new revelations in the present" (Müntzer 1993, 53). This means
that "Müntzer contends that Christians are to experience the Holy
Spirit as powerfully in postbiblical times as they did at the time of
the prophets and apostles. He insists on the baptism of the Holy
Spirit" (Burgess 2011, 142).

Although Müntzer worked as a religious and political activ-
ist, and fought for a theocracy and organized uprisings, he also
served a priest who experienced and expected the spiritual gifts
like the apostles in the New Testament. Müntzer so firmly held
these beliefs that he willing died for them on May 17, 1525 as a
martyr, beheaded by local authorities. Müntzer's life is evidence
that although some may have opposed the gift of tongues, others

experienced and taught its continuation through the sixteenth century.

Anabaptists in France & Germany (16th Century)

The Anabaptists from St. Gallen (in modern day Switzerland) practiced biblical literalism as a Protestant sect during the beginnings of the Reformation. In 1525, several years after Luther posted his ninety-five theses against the Catholic Church, their fervor for the Lord grew to such a point that they would lie down in comas together with outbursts in tongues. About five years later, they rebaptized one of their prophets along with his followers, hence the name Anabaptist. After they were rebaptized, they again experienced the gift of tongues, convulsions and other manifestations in a tent revival (Williams 1952, 132-133, 442-443). Although both the Catholics and the Protestants persecuted the Anabaptists for their odd practices; they nonetheless, demonstrated that the baptism in the Holy Spirit continued its connection to the gift of tongues.

Saint Ignatius of Loyola (16th Century)

Ignatius served as an able military leader to King Ferdinand of Spain in the wars against France. However, an accident in battle left him unable to continue military service, so he entered the ministry. Several years later, Ignatius founded a new order of priests known as the Society of Jesus, or more famously—the Jesuit Order. Ignatius also had a reputation of a deep personal intimacy with God. During his life, the Inquisition had already come to full speed and looked to squash any unorthodox practices. Therefore, Ignatius kept quiet about his experiences with the Holy Spirit. He kept a personal journal meant for his eyes only, simply called his *Spiritual Diary*.

In Ignatius' diary he frequently recorded times of intense intimacy with the Holy Spirit, followed by a phenomenon that he called *loquela*, Latin for speech, utterance, or language. The context of his use of this term implies that during his intimate times with the Holy Spirit, Ignatius spoke in tongues, but he only mentioned it in his private diary for fear of the inquisitors. The following excerpt from 1544 gives just one example of many Ignatius' entries in his diary.

> Sunday, May 11. I had tears before Mass and, during Mass too, continuous tears in great abundance. Along with them was in interior *loquela* of the Mass which to a still greater extent seemed to be given by God. On that same day I had asked for it, because during the entire week I had sometime found the exterior *loquela* and sometimes not. . . The *loquelas* of this day seemed to me very noticeably different from all of those in the past. For they came so slowly, interiorly, gently, and without noise or great motions that they seemed to arise so entirely from within that I do not know how to explain the matter. Throughout the entire duration of the interior and the exterior *loquela* everything was moving me toward divine love and the divinely granted gift of the *loquela*. Along with itself the interior *loquela* brought deep in my soul a harmony so great that I cannot express it (Ganss 1991, 267).

Saint Francis Xavier (16th Century)

Xavier, one of the founding members of the Jesuit Order, received his commission from the Pope as a missionary to India in 1539. Xavier spent most of his time ministering in the provinces and kingdoms of southern India and Sri Lanka. He also spent some time ministering in Japan. The Catholic Church reveres Xavier as one of the greatest missionaries, and Jesuit tradition claims that more than 700,000 individuals converted as a result of his ministry.

According to the Catholic Church, the secret to much of Xavier's success came from the fact that he possessed the gift of tongues. To confirm this gift, the Church sent auditors to investigate the legitimacy of Xavier's ministry. Nearly all of them came back confirming his gift and ministry after speaking with reputable first hand witnesses. The Catholic Church's biographies confirm that. . .

> Francis Xavier had this gift (tongues), which he exercised in two ways. First, he spoke the languages (which he had never learnt) of nations to whom he went to preach the gospel as freely and elegantly as if he had been born and educated in the midst of those nations; and in the second place, it not infrequently happened that men of different nations heard him at the same time, each in his own language. This happened elsewhere, and particularly in the port of (the kingdom of) Jafanapatam (on the island of Sri Lanka), and was considered as a great miracle, which made people venerate him, and also converted many (Coleridge 1876, 383).

Xavier's biographers reiterate the magnitude of his ministry's impact. Many reputable individuals in sixteenth century Asia and Europe agreed that the secret behind his powerful ministry was his gift of tongues.

The French Camisards (16th—18th Centuries)

In 1685, Louis XIV revoked the Edict of Nantes in order to quash Protestant movements in France. This change in law created fierce persecution from the king which included exile from France or even death. The Huguenots were an ethnoreligious group of French Protestants that followed the reformed theology of John Calvin. Within their ranks a zealous sect developed known as the Camisards. The Camisards fervently defended their faith with arms in order to avoid persecution or death from the king's Catholic soldiers. Though the kings' men forced this movement underground, the Camisards sparked the revival of the Protestant Church in both France and England.

The Camisards' fame also came from their gift of tongues. Due to the fact that persecution forced these men and women into hiding, their safe-houses often turned into prayer meetings where even children spoke in tongues. One such Camisard, Isabeau Vincent, was a sixteen-year-old girl who fled the persecution of the French soldiers. After fleeing to southern France, one night Vincent cried and uttered odd and incomprehensible things in her sleep. Strange manifestations took place, drawing many to come see. Vincent encouraged the people to repent and many converts gave their hearts to Jesus. After this event, Vincent had the ability to speak in the unique dialect of the southern French region which she had never learned (Villar, Pin, and Cavalier 1937, 56). In the French chronicles of the Camisards, Jacque du Bois also recorded that on January 3, 1707 in Montpellier, France, "Several persons of both sexes I have heard in their ecstasies pronounce certain words which seemed to the standards by to be some foreign language" (du Bois 1847, 152).

As a result of the French Camisard movement, John Lacy, an Englishman, who joined them wrote an interesting work titled *The General Delusion of Christians* in 1713, latter called, *The Spirit of Prophecy Defended* (Lacy 2003). Although Lacy had a tainted background, he prophesied and spoke in tongues along with other Camisards. In his book, he wrote against cessationism and defended the use of all spiritual gifts throughout the history of the Church. Lacy identified the Camisards with the Montanists of the third century (see chapter 6), and encouraged the Church to not make the same mistake twice by persecuting people filled with the Spirit.

Although many Europeans saw the Camisards as a radical fringe group, they nevertheless provide another historical example of the Church's perspective that the gift of tongues and the baptism in the Holy Spirit continued as normative Christianity.

The Jansenists (17th—18th Centuries)

Founded by Cornelius Otto Jansen, this fanatical group emigrated to different corners of Western Europe. The Jansenists faithfully followed the teachings of Augustine, a cessationist (see chapter 7). However, this group gained fame because they experienced convulsions in the Spirit, and had the ability to speak in Arabic and other languages they had never learned (Knox 1950, 372-380). Nonetheless, due to many unbiblical practices, Popes Innocent X and Alexander VII condemned and eventually destroyed this group of Catholics. Regardless of this group's odd practices, they demonstrated that the filling of the Holy Spirit and the gift of tongues continued through the seventeenth and eighteenth centuries.

The Shakers (18th Century)

The Shakers emerged from Camisard movement, but were founded in England by the Quakers, Jane and James Wardley. The Shakers founded their group under the official name, the United Society of Believers in Christ's Second Appearing, and grew in popularity in the United States when their new leader Ann Lee emigrated from England at the end of the eighteenth century. Like the Camisards, this Protestant group gained fame for quaking, shaking, or convulsing in the Spirit, hence their nickname. Also, like the Camisards and Quakers, the Shakers experienced severe persecution by other Protestants for their odd practices.

This group also shows that eighteenth century Christians possessed a sensitivity to the continuation of the filling of the Holy Spirit and the spiritual gifts, including tongues. They have historically sought the filling of the Holy Spirit and taught that the gift of tongues was not something reserved only for a few. The following historical excerpt from the Shakers exemplifies this belief system.

> The Holy Spirit was promised, and dwells in the church, with all her gifts, powers, and diversities of operation. The gifts of faith, wisdom, knowledge, discernment of spirits, gifts of healing, miracles, prophecy, tongues, and so on. All which gifts of the Holy Spirit are given to the church, for the manifestation of the Spirit—for the perfecting of the saints—for the work of the ministry—and edifying the body of Christ. . ." (Youngs 1856, 378).

John Wesley (18th Century)

Likely one of the most famous ministers in modern Church history, John Wesley, along with his brother Charles, and colleague George Whitefield, founded a movement that developed into the Methodist Church. Although Wesley remained within the Anglican Church, he determined to reform it and often challenged his leadership. Wesley did things a little differently, taking to open-air preaching when local congregations denied him entry.

Unlike many of the previous individuals or movements listed in this section of Church history, Wesley held a reputation as a biblically based man, not given to outlandish beliefs or practices. Even though there is no record where he personally practiced the gift of tongues, he fiercely defended its continuation in the Church. In his *Letter to the Reverend Dr. Conyers Middleton*, Wesley wrote. . .

> Since the Reformation, you say, "This gift [tongues] has never once been heard of, or pretended to, by the Romanists (supporters of the Roman Catholic Church) themselves." Has it "never once been heard of" since that time? Sir, your memory fails you again: It has undoubtedly been pretended to, and that at no great distance either from our time or country (Wesley 2007, 10:55).

In his personal journal, Wesley also defended the historical use of this gift among the controversial groups of the Montanists.

> I was fully convinced of what I had long suspected. 1. That the Montanists, in the second and third centuries, were real, scriptural Christians; and 2. That the grand reason why the miraculous gifts were so soon withdrawn, was not only that faith and holiness were well nigh lost; but that dry, formal, orthodox men began even then to ridicule whatever gifts they had not themselves, and to decry them as either madness or imposture (Wesley 2007, 2:204).

John Wesley also addressed the cessationist argument in order to understand why spiritual gifts had appeared to decline throughout Church history, even though they had never ceased. In his sermon *The Most Excellent Way*, Wesley preached...

> The cause of this [decline of spiritual gifts after Constantine] was not, "because there was no more occasion for them," because all the world was become Christians. This is a miserable mistake... The real cause was "the love of many," almost of all Christians, so called, was "waxed cold." The Christians had no more of the Spirit of Christ than the other Heathens (Wesley 2007, 7:27).

Conclusion

As the Reformation began to change the face of the Church, the filling of the Holy Spirit, and the gift of tongues continued. Even though some of the historical evidence includes odd practices, the historical accounts mentioned in this chapter demonstrate that both Catholics and Protestants understood that the spiritual gifts of the New Testament never stopped.

Part V

The Filling of the Holy Spirit and the Pentecostal Renewal

As the Church moved beyond the nineteenth century, much changed in world history and church doctrine. Western society passed through the enlightenment, the industrial revolution, the information revolution, modernism and postmodernism. Protestant churches and denominations birthed in the Reformation and Great Awakenings began to grow and established missionary movements across the globe. Pentecostal movements, distinct within Protestantism also began to emerge from revivals. These Pentecostal churches formed doctrines that returned to a focus on the baptism in the Holy Spirit and the gift of tongues. Part five of this book focuses on how the move of the Holy Spirit, in light of the biblical pattern, affected the Church during this time.

Chapter 10

Something New Brewing in The Church
(19th Century)

Introduction

THE NINETEENTH-CENTURY CHURCH DEMONSTRATED an increase in the historical record of the filling of the Holy Spirit and the gift of tongues. This chapter by no means develops an exhaustive historical study of the filling of the Holy Spirit, or the gift of tongues during this period. Rather it demonstrates the continuity in the historical record with the gift of tongues and the filling of the Holy Spirit as a common experience sought by a broad spectrum of individuals and cultures. As we explore historical accounts of the baptism in the Holy Spirit, and its connection to the gift of tongues, we will see that something new began to brew in the Church. The outpouring of the Holy Spirit, and the gift of tongues happened more frequently and broadly during this century, as opposed to odd and isolated incidents in centuries prior.

The Second Great Awakening

At the beginning of the nineteenth century, Charles Finney and others' preaching ministries resulted in the spread of great revival in the United States. This revival focused on many unchurched individuals who came to know Christ for the first time. Thousands of individuals, from different ethnicities, including blacks and whites, would come together for evangelistic meetings. The results of this movement affected the culture of the United States in light of personal holiness, and sparked reform for education, women's rights, and antislavery. This revival also birthed the American Bible Society, American Board for Foreign Missions, American Sunday School Union, American Tract Society, and others.

Powerful outpourings of the Holy Spirit also marked the Second Great Awakening. Manifestations of the Spirit recorded individuals convulsing, shaking, prophesying, dancing in the Spirit, being slain in the Spirit (falling over from the power of the Spirit), and speaking in tongues. Methodists and Baptists primarily organized and attended the revivals, yet these denominations no longer view the continuation of these charismatic experiences. However, this famous revival demonstrates that the baptism in the Holy Spirit, and the gift of tongues continued on a widespread basis among different social classes and ethnicities.

Saint Seraphim of Sarov

The Orthodox Church also believed in the continuation of the filling of the Spirit. Eastern Orthodoxy remembers Seraphim of Sarov, born Prokhor Moshnin, as one of the most relegated saints who greatly emphasized the Holy Spirit. Although Seraphim lived much of his life in isolation, his interactions with Russian society left a lasting impact.

Seraphim possessed the gift of prophecy. As he would emerge from his hermitry, he would answer people's questions before they would even ask them. Due to his emphasis on the Holy Spirit, Russians often attributed him with the quote, "Acquire a peaceful spirit, and thousands around you will be saved." Nikolay Motovilov, a Russian businessman and judge, wrote one of the first biographers of Seraphim. In Motovilov's conversation with Seraphim the saint stated, "Well, miserable servant of God that I am, I am going to try to explain to you what this goal is. Prayer, fasting, works of mercy—all this is very good, but it represents only the means, not the end of the Christian life. The true end is the acquisition of the Holy Spirit" (Zander 1974, 84). Although history does not record Seraphim with the gift of tongues, his account does show that the filling of the Holy Spirit continued through the nineteenth century in Russia and the Eastern Orthodox Church.

The Molokan Jumper Revival

The Molokan sect splintered from the Eastern Orthodox Church of Russia in the fifteenth century. They rejected many of the Orthodox Church traditions including many church doctrines established in early church creeds, as well as fasts on Holy Days. Instead of fasting, they would drink milk. The Molokans claim their religious heritage from the Armenian Paulicians (see chapter 7). The Church gave them the option of drinking milk during fasts in the eleventh century because their culture relied heavily on meat and milk. However, the Russian government heavily persecuted the Molokans due to their opposition to the tsar's authority.

In 1833, a revival broke out among the Molokans who lived in the Caucasus Mountain region. Many of them received the baptism in the Holy Spirit and began speaking in tongues. This group earned the name Molokan Jumpers due to their charismatic worship practices (Clay 2011). Within their practices, the Molokan Jumpers teach that the gift of tongues serves as the evidence of the baptism in the Holy Spirit. In the mid nineteenth century, Molokan presbyter, Maxin Rudametkin taught. . .

> It is possible for every liberated man to understand well that God Himself at all times personally, by His Holy Spirit, talks with nearly every member born in the bosom of His holy church not made of hands. . . of both sexes who always speak in tongues of fire through the power of the Spirit of action and utterings concerning the mysteries of God for the glory of the new coming age. . . This baptism must always be within all of us who are of one mind. And everyone of us thus baptised must have on himself a

spiritual sign, that is, the speech of the Spirit on the new tongues of fire (Rudametkin 1966, 62, 75).

Toward the end of the nineteenth century, the number of Molokans grew to an estimated half a million, at which time approximately 2,000 of the Molokan Jumpers immigrated to the United States. Many of the Molokan immigrants settled in the Los Angeles area and participated in the Pentecostal Azusa Street Revival. Today approximately 20,000 Molokans live in the former Soviet Union region, and approximately 25,000 more live mostly in the western United States.

The Scottish Revival

Edward Irving, a Scottish minister, established the Catholic Apostolic Church (different from the Roman Catholic Church). With this new movement, Irving hoped to restore what he called the five-fold ministry of apostles, prophets, evangelists, pastors, and teachers (Ephesians 4:11). He noticed that the roles of apostles and prophets were neglected by the Church and sought to revive these ministries. However, Irving himself never experienced any of the prophetic gifts and soon, his own ministry passed him over. Nevertheless, his emphasis began a movement among the Scottish people with a renewal in the charismatic gifts.

In his biography of Edward Irving, Jean Christie Root pointed out that Irving's followers returned to biblical examples of the apostles and actively sought the baptism in the Holy Spirit. As a result, they experienced outpourings of the gift of tongues and divine healing (2012). As a descendent from the Scottish Campbell clan, I was fascinated by Root's historical account of two humble families the Campbell's and the McDonalds in the Glasgow area. In Root's record, both clans had sick family members who encouraged one another and subsequently experienced the filling of the Holy Spirit, completely healed, and also spoke in tongues (Root 2012). The testimony of this account is all the more powerful because the Campbell and McDonald clans have been in a blood feud since the fourteenth century. Even today, some of these families refuse to talk with one another or even ostracize one another. However, when the Holy Spirit descended, these two families from rival clans found peace and fellowship with one another, creating an even more powerful miracle.

Simultaneous to Irving's movement another Scottish minister, by the name of James Haldane Stewart, also served in Glasgow. Under his ministry people experienced the phenomenon of speaking in other tongues, others claimed to see visions, and still others claimed to be physically healed (Shaw 1946, 34, 63-66, 68).

Following the Glasgow experience, Reverend Alexander Scott preached a sermon entitled *Charismata* in which reviving healings, tongues and prophesying began to follow. These events did not occur in isolation, rather they frequently continued as an ongoing revival until the Protestant Church of Scotland expelled these ministers. Scott and his followers splintered from the Protestant Church to form part of the Catholic Apostolic Church with Edward Irving; there they continued to experience the same manifestations of the Holy Spirit (Shaw 1946, 34-35).

John Evangelist George Lutz

Lutz served as a Roman Catholic Priest in nineteenth century Germany. In 1838 a revival broke out in Father Lutz's parish where his parishioners claimed to have spoken in other tongues, prophesied, had visions, and spoke of Christ's second coming. They also spoke of the restoration of the spiritual gifts from the early church similar to those from Edward Irving's movement in Scotland (Schöler 1894, 30-34). This experience adds to the evidence that something new began to happen in the Church. Christians sought the baptism in the Holy Spirit, and the common response came in the gift of tongues.

Horace Bushnell

While charismatic revivals took place in Scotland and Germany, across the Atlantic in the United States, New Englanders also experienced the filling of the Holy Spirit and spoke in tongues. Graduate of Yale Divinity School, and Congregationalist minister, Horace Bushnell gave a theologically academic defense for the continuation of the baptism in the Holy Spirit and the gift of tongues. Bushnell argued that the cessationist position on charismatic gifts was hollow and lazy, because it could not explain the supernatural and based its defense on one's own lack of experience of the gifts. He stated. . .

> If miracles are inherently incredible, which is the impression at the root of our modern unbelief, evidently nothing is gained by thrusting them back into remote ages of time. If, on the other hand, they are inherently credible, why treat them as if they were not? Raising ingenious and forced hypotheses to account for their non-occurrence? (Bushnell 1858, 445).

In his scholarly defense, Bushnell continued to cite many of the same historical examples listed in this book as evidence that the charismatic gifts did indeed continue throughout Church history. Bushnell's biblical and scholarly defense of the connection between the baptism in the Holy Spirit and the gift of tongues, established a legitimate doctrinal position.

Revival in India

While Pentecostal revival began among Catholics and Protestants in Europe and America, the Holy Spirit simultaneously worked across the globe in India. John Christian Aroolappen was born in southern India and raised as a Catholic. Due to influence from Protestant missionaries from Germany, England, and Prussia, Aroolappen converted to Protestantism. As news of the charismatic revivals in the west reached India, Aroolappen and other believers began to seek the baptism in the Holy Spirit. In his diary, Aroolappen stated. . .

> On the 18th May, [1860], the Lord met most of my people by pouring out His Holy Spirit. In the month of June some of our people praised the Lord by unknown tongues, with their interpretations. In the month of July the Spirit was poured out upon our congregation at Oleikollam, and about 25 persons were baptized by one of my sons-in-law and two other brothers who labour among them. . . Then my son and daughter and three others went to visit their own relations. . . They also received the Holy Ghost. Some prophecy, some speak by known tongues with their interpretations (Aroolappen 1939, 144).

Conclusion

The common charismatic experiences of the nineteenth century encompassed a broad spectrum of the globe, both sexes, among various ages and ethnicities. The historical record reveals that the baptism in the Holy Spirit occurred more frequently among peoples of various Christian faiths: Catholic, Orthodox, Protestant, and many denominations or sects thereof. This new brewing of the Holy Spirit prepared the way for the global Pentecostal revivals in the following centuries.

Chapter 11

The Pentecostal Revival
(20th—21st Centuries)

Introduction

THE TWENTIETH, AND TWENTY-FIRST centuries have seen techno-
logical advances, and cross-cultural globalization at an exponential
level compared to previous centuries. Transportation, and communication have advanced to such a degree that they have nearly
eradicated cultural isolation. These advancements have also created virtually instantaneous contact between cultures, groups, and
individuals from any point of the globe. Therefore, it should not
surprise us that in a little more than a century, revivals and missionary movements have spread world-wide. This chapter builds
on the context of globalization. Revivals began to expand beyond
regional or political boarders. Church movements revived the
New Testament pattern of living in the Spirit, and the Pentecostal
movement of Spirit-empowered believes have grown as one of the
largest Christian movements today.

Volumes of books have been written on the Pentecostal outpouring that sparked at the beginning of the twentieth century;
to address them all would go far beyond the scope of this chapter. Therefore, I focus primarily on key examples of this revival

to understand its connection to the biblical experience, Church history, and the implications for the Church today.

The Catholic Charismatic Renewal

At the turn of the twentieth century Elena Guerra, a Catholic Italian nun, wrote a series of letters to Pope Leo XIII. In her letters she stressed the lack of emphasis on the Holy Spirit in the Catholic Church and urged the Pope to use his authority to initiate a *Novena* (renewal) for Pentecost. In her first letter, she boldly stated, "Who, Oh Holy Father, can do the Holy Spirit well-known and more honored, but the Vicar of Jesus on earth, which not only the orders, but also the desires, have on the heart of the faithful a strong effectiveness?" (Guerra 1895). Two years after Sister Elena began sending letters, Pope Leo XIII issued a global decree for all Catholics in his *Divinum Illud Munus*, stating. . .

> We ought to pray to and invoke the Holy Spirit, for each one of us greatly needs His protection and His help. . . We decree and command that throughout the whole Catholic Church, this year and in every subsequent year, a Novena shall take place before Whit-Sunday, in all parish churches, and also, if the local Ordinaries think fit, in other churches and oratories (Leo XIII 1897).

This renewed emphasis on the filling of the Holy Spirit paved the way for many significant changes within the Catholic Church especially with regard to the gift of tongues. In 1962, Pope John XXIII called for *The Second Ecumenical Council of the Vatican*, also known as *Vatican II*. This unparalleled meeting allowed for major changes in many Catholic doctrines. Moreover, this unprecedented meeting also allowed and invited Protestant and Orthodox Church leaders to observe. The meetings lasted until 1965 under the leadership of the new Pope, Paul VI.

Among the many significant changes and reforms within the Church, one significant document resulted, *Lumen Gentium* (Light of the Nations). In this document, Pope Paul VI wrote on behalf of the Catholic Church affirming "It is not only through the sacraments and ministries of the Church that the Holy Spirit sanctifies and leads the people of God and enriches it with virtues, but 'allotting his gifts to everyone according as He wills'" (Paul VI 1964). This significant change in Catholic theology transformed the Church's traditional doctrine which assumed that only a select few saintly individuals were worthy enough to possess the gift of tongues.

A decade later, Pope Paul VI spoke to the Catholic Charismatic Renewal group and affirmed that "the Church and the World need more than ever that 'the miracle of Pentecost should be continued in history'... How then could this 'spiritual renewal' be other than a blessing for the Church and for the World?.... All spiritual gifts are to be received gratefully" (Paul VI 2000, 18-22). Pope John Paul II went a step further when he addressed the same group alluding to the fact that he also operated in the charismatic gifts; though he did not specify. He stated...

> I have always belonged to this renewal in the Holy Spirit. . . so I can understand all the different charisms. All of them are part of the riches of the Lord. I am convinced that this movement is a sign of his action. The world is much in need of this action of the Holy Spirit, and it needs many instruments for this action. . . I am convinced that this movement is a very important component in the total renewal of the Church (John Paul II 2000, 76-77).

Church history reveals that neither the filling of the Holy Spirit, nor the gift of tongues ever ceased. However, since the dawn of the twentieth century, a charismatic revival has significantly shaped Catholics who have experienced the baptism in the Holy Spirit, and the gift of tongues.

Even from the twentieth to the twenty-first century, the Papal office has maintained an open stance to the charismatic gifts of the Holy Spirit. Both John Paul II, and his successor Benedict XVI appointed Raniero Cantalamessa, a distinguished Italian Catholic professor who holds multiple doctorates, as special preacher to the

Papal office. Cantalamessa regularly preached to the leadership of the Catholic Church and published profound statements on the baptism in the Holy Spirit in his work, *Come, Creator Spirit: Meditations on the Veni Creator*. He stated, . . .

> I believe that we aught certainly to encourage people to be open to this gift [tongues], and to use it, especially in the area of personal prayer. . . In Pentecostal and charismatic gatherings, this is a gift quite beautiful in its simplicity. It allows us to transcend the limitation of set words and known melodies, and in so doing, it creates a real unity of heart and should throughout the entire assembly. It is a wonderful expression of adoration, praise, rejoicing and thanksgiving to God, majestic in its tranquility (Cantalamessa 2003, 224-225).

The Birth of Classical Pentecostalism and the Azusa Street Revival

At the turn of the twentieth century when Sister Elena Guerra and Pope Leo XIII initiated a charismatic renewal among Catholics, Charles Parham did the same among Protestants in Topeka, Kansas. Parham came from a Methodist background highly influenced by the Holiness movement. He also held a deep passion for missions. In 1898 he rented a small space in Topeka to run a Bible School that would train missionaries. Parham focused on the work of the Holy Spirit and the need to fulfill the Great Commission. On January 1, 1901, Agnes Ozman, one of Parham's students sought the baptism in the Holy Spirit and began to speak in tongues. Soon after Parham and nearly all of his students experienced the filling of the Holy Spirit, and also spoke in tongues. Parham's wife, Sarah, recounted the powerful experience stating. . .

> Twelve ministers of different denominations, who were in the school, were filled with the Holy Spirit and spoke with other tongues. Some were sitting, some still kneeling, other standing with hands upraised. . . When I beheld the evidence of the restoration of Pentecostal power, my

> heart was melted in gratitude to God for what my eyes had seen. . . I fell to my knees behind a table unnoticed by those upon whom the power of Pentecost had fallen to pour my heart out to God in thanksgiving. . . Right then there came a slight twist in my throat, a glory fell over me, and I began to worship God in the Swedish tongue, which later changed to other languages and continued so until the morning (Parham 1944, 52-53).

Church historians credit Parham with the establishment of the classical Pentecostal movement and the Pentecostal doctrine of tongues as the initial physical evidence of the baptism in the Holy Spirit. A few years later, Parham established another school in Houston with a black Holiness preacher by the name of Willian Seymour. Later, Seymour moved to Los Angeles and began the famed Azusa Street Revival in 1906. Influenced by the Holiness movement, and the Pentecostal preaching from Parham, Seymour began to preach and many individuals began speaking in tongues with interpretations. Prophecies followed along with confirmed healings. At first mostly blacks filled the old African Methodist Episcopal Church building; however, soon after whites and other ethnicities came, breaking major racial stigmas. The revival gained such fame that it lasted for three years and people from across the globe came. Many Pentecostal movements in other countries, including Brazil, and Korea trace their roots to the Azusa Street Revival. Seymour summed up this experience for those who wish to seek it in his *Letter to One Seeking the Holy Ghost.* . .

> After we were clearly sanctified, we prayed to God for the baptism with the Holy Spirit. So he sent the Holy Spirit to our hearts and filled us with His blessed Spirit, and He gave us the Bible evidence, according to the 2nd chapter of Acts verses 1 to 4, speaking with other tongues as the Spirit gives utterance. Praise our God, He is the same yesterday, today, and forever. Receive Him just now and He will fill you. Amen. Don't get discouraged but pray until you are filled (Seymour 1907, 3).

The Growth of Pentecostal/Charismatic Churches

Most of the Pentecostal or Charismatic Christian denominations trace their roots to the Azusa Street Revival. This revival even influenced the Catholic Charismatic Renewal to some degree. Although the Church of God was one of the first Pentecostal denominations, founded in Tennessee in 1886 before the Azusa Street Revival, much of its growth was later influenced by Azusa Street. Today the Church of God has an international presence with more than seven million adherents (Church of God).

In 1911, the International Pentecostal Holiness Church formed as a merger of churches from the Holiness movement and the Methodist Episcopal Church as a result of the Pentecostal revival of Azusa Street. Currently the movement consists of a constituency of more than four and a half million people in more than 100 nations (International Pentecostal Holiness Church).

The Assemblies of God, formed in Arkansas 1914, also as fruit from the Azusa Street Revival. Consisting primarily of churches and ministers rejected by their denominations because they had received the gift of tongues, they formed a cooperative fellowship with the purpose of the "greatest evangelism that the world has ever seen" (General Council of the Assemblies of God 1914, 12). The third Assemblies of God General Superintendent, John Welch, evoked this notion in the early years of the denomination when he stated that the "the General Council of the Assemblies of God was never meant to be an institution, it is just a missionary agency" (Welch 1920, 8). Today the Assemblies of God has grown to become the largest Pentecostal denomination in America (General Council of the Assemblies of God). Despite the fact that many other denominations have suffered decline, the Assemblies of God continues to expand at a growth rate that has almost equated to starting one new church every day (Banks 2012). Similarly, the growth trend continued worldwide where the Assemblies of God developed into the largest denomination among all Protestants (Belief Bits 2017). As of 2017, the denomination consists of a constituency of over sixty-eight and a half million individuals in nearly every country on earth (Assemblies of God World Missions 2017). Many attribute this growth, both domestic and abroad, to the foundational principle that the Assemblies formed over missions. However, many would also attribute this growth to a denomination that relies on the power of the Holy Spirit to fulfill its part in the Great Commission.

In 1923, Assemblies of God pastor, Aimee Semple McPherson, wanted to start a global mission's movement. Her emphasis grew rapidly into the International Church of the Foursquare Gospel, a Pentecostal denomination with an international influence of more than eight and a half million members in 144 countries (International Church of the Foursquare Gospel 2017).

These Pentecostal denominations serve as a sample of the explosion of Pentecostal/Charismatic churches across the world. This movement emphasizes a renewal of intimacy with God, an empowerment of the Holy Spirit to fulfill the Great Commission, and an expectation of the evidence of that fulfillment with the gift of tongues. The Pew Research Center found there to be more than 700 Pentecostal or Charismatic denominations with more than 500 million adherents across the globe (Pew Center Research 2011). In just over a century, the Church has been impacted with a revival of the outpouring of the Holy Spirit like never before.

Eastern Pentecostal Revivals

Pandita Ramabai lived as an Indian reformer and worked for women's rights. Born into the highest caste of a Brahman family and raised in Hinduism, she eventually converted as an Evangelical Christian due to contact with missionaries who gave her a Bible. After traveling to England and the United States she returned to Khedgaon, India and established a mission. Her mission focused on reaching those rejected by society such as the physically disabled, orphans, and prostitutes. In 1905 during a regular prayer meeting Ramabai began seeking the Holy Spirit. During the meeting she, and hundreds of her followers, began to speak in tongues. She recounted the experience stating. . .

I was led by the Lord to start a special prayer-circle at the beginning of 1905. There were about 70 of us who met together each morning, and prayed for the true conversion of the Indian Christians including ourselves, and for a special outpouring of the Holy Spirit on all Christians of every land. In six months from the time we began to pray in this manner, the Lord graciously sent a glorious Holy Ghost revival among us, and also in many schools and Churches in this country. . . Many hundreds of our girls and some of our boys have been gloriously saved, and many of them are serving God, and witnessing for Christ at home, and in other places (Ramabai 2000, 320).

Change in Opinion of Many Evangelical Churches

Without a doubt the Pentecostal revivals that occurred throughout the twentieth century have received their fair share of criticism. Unfortunately, many churches, pastors, and individuals have struggled to adequately explain their experience with comprehensive biblical or historical support. Therefore, in 1927 George Barton Cutten, a Yale educated psychologist, and president of Colgate University in Hamilton, New York, became one of the first and few to give the modern tongues experience and Pentecostal revival an academic defense. In his book, *Speaking with Tongues: Historically and Psychologically Considered*, Cutten begins with a psychological understanding, . . .

> Speaking with tongues is an experience which most people believe to be confined to apostolic times and bestowed as a special favor on a few followers of Jesus. . . It may seem that, when a person stands up to speak, it is not the utterance but the thinking back of the utter, which causes the strain. With those who find even rudimentary thought difficult, speech of an intelligent nature cannot long progress, the thinking process soon refusing to function; and when, owing to the ease of operation and the suggestion to action, speech continues after thought is exhausted, a series of meaningless syllables

results. This is the Pauline type of speaking with tongues
(Cutten 1927, 1, 4).

Due to the powerful and controversial revivals in the early
twentieth century, Cutten continued to help understand the setting. He noted that the revivals such as Azusa Street demonstrated
that individuals did not seek the gift of tongues as fervently since
the Day of Pentecost. Cutten further explained the psychological
misconceptions of tongues in its historical settings. His greatest
concern came with the middle ages where mysticism reigned,
and individuals could easily pass off ecstatic speech as some sort
of witchcraft because they did not understand it. Therefore, the
literature from such times is often skewed or limited (Cutten
1927, 134).

Some still continue with the cessationist doctrine and teach
against the baptism in the Holy Spirit and tongues. However, many
denominations and independent churches have come to recognize the biblical patterns, the historical evidence, and the legitimacy today that link the filling of the Holy Spirit, and prophecy
or tongues. Many denominations that held positions against any
form of charismatic expression at the beginning of the twentieth
century are now sympathetic or open to Pentecostal or charismatic
expressions.

Conclusion

I began this timeline with Job and Moses in the patriarchal era of
the Old Testament nearly 4,000 years ago. Before Christ died on
the cross, when the Holy Spirit would fill an individual the biblical
pattern came as a prophetic expression. After Christ fulfilled the
law by his sacrifice on the cross, the Holy Spirit poured himself out
on all people; however, the biblical pattern of prophetic utterance
continued in the form of tongues—*the* gift of the Spirit as Peter
called it. Although Church history displays some odd doctrines
that have come and gone over the centuries, it also demonstrates
that neither the baptism in the Holy Spirit, nor the Spirit's gift of

tongues ever ceased. Therefore, Christians today should neither expect this experience to cease. The empowerment of the Holy Spirit exists to fulfill the task of the Great Commission which would be impossible without his baptism (Acts 1:8; Matthew 29:19-20; Mark 16:15-20). The Great Commission will never come to an end until Christ's return; thus, the Prophet Joel and the Apostle Peter affirmed that this outpouring of the Spirit will continue throughout the last days (Joel 2:28-32; Acts 2:16-21)

Chapter 12

Implications

So What's This Mean for Me Today?

Introduction

IN LIGHT OF THE biblical and historical pattern that connects the filling of the Holy Spirit to prophetic utterance, I dedicate one final chapter to some practical implications for today. Many people remain skeptical of the prophetic gifts, especially tongues. Such skepticism is completely normal because it reflects a supernatural experience. However, we must remain careful to not disregard this gift just because it is weird (and yes, it is a little weird). There are plenty of weird things in the Bible, but that does not mean that they are illegitimate, rather that they are beyond normal. The gift of tongues is not normal or natural in any way, in fact it is supernatural which makes it a divine gift. If the gift of tongues were normal, then it could not serve as a sign or a gift at all because it would be something that people could, and would do naturally.

My point in the biblical and historical journey that this book takes is to show, that prophecy, and more specifically prophecy in the form of tongues, serves as a pattern that God has placed as a subsequent experience to the filling of the Holy Spirit. This experience confirms something that God has already done on the inside, empowered his people to fulfil their part in his will. Just like baptism in water is an exterior sign of an interior experience, the evidence is the fact that you get wet. Similarly, the baptism in the Holy Spirit gives external evidence of an internal experience, found in the gift of tongues.

In an attempt to understand this supernatural experience, this chapter explores a unique perspective on the gift of tongues from a linguist and theologian. This perspective helps to develop some communication theory insight in light of the theology of the gift of tongues. The second half of this chapter focuses on seven major barriers that generally inhibit individuals from the experience of the baptism in the Holy Spirit, many of which generally occur subconsciously.

A Linguist's Perspective on the Gift of Tongues

In his book, *The Foolishness of God: A Linguist Looks at the Mystery of Tongues*, Dr. Del Tarr applies communication theory to the concept of tongues (Tarr 2012). His work is based on the perceived ridiculousness of the concept of tongues and applies it to Paul's statement, "For the foolishness of God is wiser than man's wisdom, and the weakness of God is stronger than man's strength" (1 Corinthians 1:25). Tarr makes the point that the wisdom of God in using our tongue, proves his divine intervention in the lives of men. God chose the tongue because it distinguishes man from beast, and because man has never been able to tame the tongue (James 3:1-12). The world sees this amazing, powerful, and wise act as foolishness, but when we really think about it, foolishness for God goes beyond wisdom for man, for his ways are so much higher than our ways (Isaiah 55:8-9).

> We use our minds (superior among all God's creatures) to justify our grand rebellion against God and His ways, by recreating God in OUR own image. Similarly, in mankind's upside-down thinking, the secular world took Darwin's theory as their gospel because it allowed mankind to get rid of the judge (Bretscher 1964, 82).

If we are to be honest, we like things understandable, normal, explainable, and measurable. In this attempt to put God in a box, we consider anything that does not fit into our understanding as weird and foolish. Therefore, we develop an upside down mentality to justify things as we think they should function, yet that does not necessarily reflect reality. We may not like gravity, and cannot see it, but that does not mean that it does not exist. The same is true for God's divine activity; we may not be able to understand it completely, but that does not mean that it does not exist either. Unfortunately, like the Corinthian church, there are plenty of people who abuse this gift and make tongues even weirder than it really is. Therefore, this section addresses this issue with a scientific approach through the lens of linguistics.

Since the time of the patriarchs in the Old Testament, God has chosen a prophetic response as a sign of the move of his Spirit on mankind. For approximately four millennia, and in nearly every culture that has had men and women of God, this response has appeared, and in many cases, independently of others. Today more than 584 million individuals identify themselves as Charismatic or Pentecostal (Center for the Study of Global Christianity 2011). This means that 27% of the 2.2 billion Christians in the world have experienced this same phenomenon (Pew Research Center 2017). Therefore, theologically, sociologically, and linguistically, we cannot ignore this experience. Nevertheless, individuals have historically ignored and strongly criticized this very biblical experience. Tarr proposes two logical reasons for this rejection. The first deals with issues of power; the second deals with issues of philosophy.

In regard to issues of power, Morton Kelsey proposed a key point stating, "There is always tension between those who stand for individual experience and those who stand for ecclesiastical authority. . . This same tension accounts for much of the modern rejection of tongues" (Kelsey 1968, 159). When an individual receives a prophetic gift such as tongues, that prophecy by definition is communication inspired by God. Therefore, a church organization, whether the Catholic Church, a Protestant denomination, or a local church as an institution naturally finds itself in conflict with the individual. The authority of the church institution comes into question when the individual essentially goes over their head by dealing directly with God. Who wouldn't feel threatened by that? Unfortunately, when church institutions base their authority on the institution itself, major problem result because they, as the leaders can no longer hold influence when an individual experiences a prophetic utterance. Therefore, since the formal organization of the Church under Constantine in the fourth century (see chapter 7), many church leaders have fought against the concept of the prophetic gifts. Many of these same leaders also taught the cessation of these gifts with the death of the apostles. From the twelfth century until the 1960's, the Catholic Church has limited the gift of tongues, teaching that only saints can have such abilities. This doctrine conveniently allows the leadership of a church or denomination to eliminate any question to their authoritarian teachings or control.

However, churches can manage the issue of power or influence in a healthy manner. An anarchical response to the issue of power is by no means a realistic or healthy response. Church leadership is a biblical principle, but we must orient ourselves correctly to such power and authority. When the Spirit speaks, and prophecy follows, church authorities should help their parishioners understand how to receive and test such expression within biblical parameters. When the Bible takes the place as the ultimate authority (*sola scriptura*), and churches us it as the measuring and managing tool for all prophetic utterance, the Church will be edified. Such practices will also help church leadership minimize and avoid many of the damages of the abuse of these charismatic gifts, one of Paul's great concerns with the believers in the church at Corinth.

In regard to philosophy, protestant and Catholic movements come from a western perspective. Tarr contends that western philosophy of communication primarily comes from Aristotle's teachings in his *Rhetoric*. Aristotle's teachings come from a rationalist and linear thought-process. Although Plato, Aristotle's mentor, allowed room for the intervention of the supernatural, Aristotle held the conviction that logic must reign. The emerging western church adopted Aristotle's philosophies which left little room for supernatural, extraordinary, or divine activity.

> Theology has accented the logica of faith and thus has been ill-equipped to respond to the kind of dynamic pneumatic experience that borders on the non-rational. Theology has served only to shun and stifle the creative manifestations of the Spirit, which continue to be a 'bug-bear' for theologians (Macchia 1992, 49-50).

Management of truncated philosophies likens to learning other units of measurement. Many Americans use the imperial system of measurement with miles, yards, feet, inches, gallons, quarts, cups, pounds, ounces, etc. However, the vast majority of the world functions on the metric system of kilometers, liters, kilograms, etc. Whether imperial or metric, Fahrenheit or Celsius, adapting from something different never comes easily. This does not mean that one is better or worse than the other, rather they simply reflect different systems and different perspectives of measurement. However, to assume that there is only one way to measure would be immature.

Similarly, individuals who were raised with one philosophical system of western theology, based Aristotle's logical and linear perspective, struggle to see the world, Scripture, or God in any other way. This does not mean that this philosophy or theology is wrong, but it is naïve to presume that it is the only perspective, and dangerously myopic to assume that any other perspectives are wrong. God is much bigger than human comprehension. Even though change creates difficulties we must learn to look beyond our own small philosophies to the vastness that the Bible shows in relation to God's divine interaction with humanity.

Therefore, when individuals can accept that God works far outside of our comprehension or philosophy, we can begin to see beyond our narrow and limited view of God. We can also begin to understand the beautiful balance between the guidance of his ordained leaders in the Church, and the move of his Spirit upon individuals. We may finally realize that our theology may not be wrong *per se*, but it may be only one limited way of looking at our Divine Creator and his methodology to interact with humanity. Although we may struggle to look beyond the issues of authority and philosophy, it is not impossible. However, once we can look beyond these issues, we begin to see the barriers that we have in our own lives in regard to the activity of the Holy Spirit. Both sociologists and linguists understand that language reflects one's culture and philosophy; tongues does not differ. The theological perspective that an individual has to *the gift of the Spirit*, as Peter called it, reflects their preconceived values and ideas.

Common Barriers to the Baptism in the Holy Spirit

Tongues accompanies the baptism in the Holy Spirit as an evidential gift. However, a gift cannot merely be given, it must also be received. Many individuals ask, "why don't I speak in tongues? Why don't I receive the baptism in the Holy Spirit?" We must remember first of all that we don't determine the giving of the gift, the Spirit determines when and to whom to give spiritual gifts (1 Corinthians 2:11). However, on the receiving end, we must also understand that different reasons, albeit even subconscious reasons, cause us to refuse the gift even when the Spirit gives it. In this section I propose seven specific reasons (although this list is not all-encompassing) that cause individuals to refuse what the Spirit offers, the inspiration for the first five came from evangelist Rob Enloe (2013).

1. Anti-Pentecostal Baggage

This mentality comes from an underlying fear of a counterfeit experience. From a young age, many people erroneously learned that the gift of tongues comes from the devil, or that the gift is not biblical. Therefore, they understandably refuse to seek the baptism in the Holy Spirit, let alone open their mouths, lest they actually speak in tongues. Such a perspective also creates fear and dissention among Christians, developing an "us vs. them" mentality.

One of the most effective ways to overcome such a mentality or fear comes when individuals ground themselves in the Word of God. One of the purposes of this book is to do exactly that—show individuals that the filling of the Holy Spirit and prophetic utterance is extremely biblical and has been God's *modus operandi* from the beginning. When individuals understand how biblical this experience is, they will begin to lower their guard and open themselves to receive all that God has for them. Once individuals understand that the Holy Spirit also meant this biblical experience for them, they will more readily seek it. This is why Jesus said, . . .

> Which of you father, if your son asks for a fish, will give
> him a snake instead? Or if he asks for an egg, will give
> him a scorpion? If you then, though you are evil, know
> how to give good gifts to your children, how much more
> will your Father in heaven give the Holy Spirit to those
> who ask him! (Luke 11:11-13).

2. Shy or Introverted Personality

This mentality comes from the fear of humiliation or public attention and commonly creates barriers to receive the baptism in the Holy Spirit. Unfortunately, churches regularly ask individuals in a service to come forward to receive the baptism. Of course the baptism experience could happen in such a setting, but it creates a mentality that individuals have to go somewhere to receive it. This mentality also creates difficulties for introverts who often struggle with public attention. So why do we think that they will to receive the baptism in the Holy Spirit in the front of a church full of people, when they are afraid to walk down to the front without shaking in their boots?

An effective way to help individuals overcome this barrier is to encourage them to find a private place to pray, or if they are in church, pray right where they are. They can even whisper their prayer privately. This privacy removes unnecessary social pressure and allows them to relax and receive what the Lord has for them. It also helps individuals know that they can receive the baptism at home, as was the case for my wife. Many individuals have testified that they received Spirit baptism in the shower, probably because it is the one place they don't have distractions. I have even heard of one person receiving it while riding his bicycle! The point is to not create a show. We must orientate our hearts and attitudes in order to willing receive what the Spirit has to offer.

3. Hyper Analytical

This mentality comes from the fear of not understanding or intellectually processing what your experience. I personally struggled with this barrier. As an analytical person, I struggle when I cannot explain something. Many individuals also struggle with the baptism in the Holy Spirit and its accompanying gift—tongues, because it comes as a supernatural experience we cannot easily explain.

To overcome this barrier, I suggest we put our "analyzer" on hold first, and willingly receive what God has, and then analyze the experience afterward. I do not advocate "not thinking", but rather willingly allow God to work and not think, "We'll, I've been standing here for the last 45 minutes and I feel like I am going to fall over, and now I have a cold chill on my neck, but that is because I am sweating and they just turned on the fans." Sometimes we get in our own way and over analyze things. Therefore, in this case, I propose we do things in reverse order, where we open ourselves up to receive first, recognizing that we cannot fully explain spiritually abstract concepts, and then analyze the experience afterward. The idea is that hyper analytical people typically lead with their head and follow with their heart. I suggest making an effort to do the reverse of leading with your heart and then following with your head to overcome this barrier.

4. The Passive Approach

This mentality comes from a fear of self-inducement of a counterfeit experience; and therefore, we assume it is not divine. Individuals who struggle with this area fear that either they just made something up in their head, or they wait for the Holy Spirit to possess them and move their mouth like a puppet.

To overcome this barrier, we must first understand communication theory in God's design. The apostle Paul helps us understand this very concept when he gave the Corinthian Church guidelines for the prophetic experience of the Spirit baptism. In regard to the evidence of the baptism in the Holy Spirit, Paul reminded the Corinthians that the prophetic gift of tongues requires an act of obedience and control by the speaker. He stated, "The spirits of prophets are subjects to the control of prophets" (1 Corinthians 14:32), and finished his thought encouraging them by stating, "be eager to prophesy, and do not forbid speaking in tongues. But everything should be done in a fitting and orderly way" (vv. 39-40).

When God gave prophetic messages to individuals to speak, or to write in the case of the biblical text, he gave them a message in their mind and they had to obey and open their mouth or pick up a pen. Tongues works in much the same way. Tongues are a type of prophecy. The syllables come to the mind of the speaker from the Holy Spirit. However, the speaker remains in control; therefore, he doesn't make up what comes out of his mouth. We must also understand that Holy Spirit will not move your mouth, which means we must act in obedience to work in cooperation with the Spirit—it is a partnership.

5. Overwhelming Feelings of Unworthiness

This mentality comes from the fear of rejection. A great fear for people who seek the baptism in the Holy Spirit, is that God will pass by them, they won't be good enough, or maybe they will be the only ones that will not receive the baptism. Many times individuals come forward for prayer seeking the Spirit's baptism and nothing happens, so they develop overwhelming feelings of unworthiness because they feel like they have been passed over again. Others erroneously assume that speaking in tongues reflects some sort of spiritual maturity, and assume that if they don't speak in tongues, the Spirit does not consider them spiritually mature enough.

An effective way to help overcome this barrier lies in the assurance that Jesus is worthy and supplies all the worthiness in every spiritual transaction. We don't deserve anything, but live and operate in the mercy and grace of Jesus. When we realize who we are in him, and what the Spirit wants to do through us, feelings of unworthiness begin to fade away along with the barriers to receive all that God has for us. For those who assume tongues serve as a sign of spiritual maturity, we must remember that the Holy Spirit determines when and where individuals receive the baptism experience and its accompanying gift. Paul's letters to the Corinthian Church give evidence to realize that spiritual maturity has nothing to do with the baptism experience. The Bible does not make that connection, and the Corinthians obviously struggled with the use of a gift they had due to their spiritual immaturity. One of Paul's most powerful statements related to this very issue reminds us that, "God made him who had no sin to be sin for us, so that in him we might become the righteousness of God" (2 Corinthians 5:21).

6. Seeking the Gift Rather than the Giver

This mentality comes from the desire to receive the gift of speaking in tongues rather than on intimacy with the Giver himself. Many people fall into the same error as Simon the Sorcerer (Acts 8:18-19). People become mesmerized by the glamor of tongues, and like Simon, desire the evidence rather than the actual baptismal experience. Since tongues are a gift, then we should not seek the gift with selfish intentions, rather we should seek the Holy Spirit and allow him to give when he determines (1 Corinthians 12:11). James warned those who seek with mal intent stating, . . .

> You want something but don't get it. You kill and covet, but you cannot have what you want. You quarrel and fight. You do not have, because you do not ask God. When you ask, you do not receive, because you ask with wrong motives, that you may spend what you get on your pleasures (James 4:2-3).

At a young age, my wife, Marj found herself mesmerized by this gift. She saw individuals in her church receive the baptism in the Holy Spirit and speak in tongues. Her infatuation with the gift made her desire it. She would come forward on a regular basis at the end of a church service for prayer and constantly seek the gift of tongues, but to no avail. She would consistently leave disappointed until an elderly sister in the church helped her. She encouraged Marj to stop seeking the gift and begin to seek the Giver himself. She likened it to a child who seeks a toy from their parents versus a child who just seeks intimacy with their parents. Not long after Marj began to re-orient her perspective did she find herself alone at home, seeking the Lord when something different and beautiful began to pour from her lips as she prayed.

To effectively overcome this barrier, we must stop seeking the gift. Don't come to a church service hoping that some big-name preacher will do something for you. Remember that Jesus sends the Holy Spirit (John 16:7), and the Holy Spirit gives the gifts (1 Corinthians 12:11). Seek God!

7. Assuming that any Gift or Spiritual Experience is the Baptism

Many people see others who are "slain in the Spirit", which doesn't even appear in the Bible. Others see people who "tremble in the Spirit", which really doesn't happen in the Bible either, at least in this kind of a context, and in some cases may even serve as a sign of demon possession (Matthew 17:14-21). Still others say that any spiritual gift can serve as the sign of the baptism in the Holy Spirit, and others say that we all received the Spirit baptism at salvation.

We must remember we are social creatures. We see something and we believe it as a legitimate experience, so we copy it. We must stop making it an emotional experience and make it a spiritual experience. Even though the move of the Spirit can stir emotions, remember that emotions are not the point. We don't have to fall in the Spirit or shake. These things can happen, but many times they happen because of emotions and not because of the Spirit's baptism.

In regard to the evidence, we must return to the Bible. The only biblical patter of the filling of the Spirit is prophetic, and more specifically in the form of tongues in the New Testament. The Bible does not give us the license to connect any other experience apart from tongues to the baptism in the Holy Spirit.

In regard to receiving the baptism in the Holy Spirit in the moment of salvation. It can happen, as was the case for Cornelius and his household (Acts 10:44-46). However, it does not have to happen that way. Obviously we don't receive God in stages or parts, we must remember to distinguish the Holy Spirit from the baptism experience. The baptism in the Holy Spirit is a subsequent event that empowers believers to fulfil their part in the Great Commission (Acts 1:8).

Conclusion

We must remember that neither the baptism experience, nor tongues are a one-time event, but a process, and this may be a journey that God has put us on. This all boils down to the fact that God wants to give you power to do what he is calling you to do. It is really basic. The question is, will you be willing to allow God to use you and respond? The speaking in tongues is just the prophetic evidence that the Spirit has come upon and empowered you. Really, you're allowing him to speak through you, submitting the most untamable part of your body to him—your tongue. This experience is something vital to your call. It is something that God wants us to seek. However, many people resist it because it is different, strange, or unfamiliar. This experience was a command of Christ and the last thing he said to his disciples (ref. Acts 1:4-9). God wants to use you. Will you let him?

Bibliography

Aroolappen, John Christian. *The History and Diaries of an Indian Christian*. G. H. Lang ed. London: Thynne. 1939.

Assemblies of God World Missions. *AGWM Vital Stats, no. 3*. https://agwm. com/assets/agwmvitalstats.pdf (accessed August 11, 2017).

Banks, Adelle. Assemblies of God Starts a Church a Day. *Christianity Today –Live Blog* (January, 2012). http://www.christianitytoday.com/gleanings/2012/january/assemblies-of-god-starts-church-day.html (accessed September 17, 2017).

Belief Bits. http://www.888c.com/WorldChristianDenominations.htm (accessed September 17, 2017).

Bray, Gerald. "Basil of Caesarea, The Long Rules 7" in *1-2 Corinthians: Ancient Christian Commentary Series*. Thomas Oden, trans. 3rd ed. Downers Grove, IL: InterVarsity. 1999.

Bretscher, Paul. *The World Upside-Down or Right-Side Up?* Saint Louis, MO: Concordia.1964.

Burgess, Stanley. *Christian Peoples of the Spirit: A Documentary History of Pentecostal Spirituality from the Early Church to Present*. New York: New York University Press. 2011.

Bushnell, Horace. *Nature and the Supernatural as together Constituting the One System of God*. New York: Scribner. 1858.

Cantalamessa, Raniero. *Come, Creator Spirit: Meditations on the Veni Creator*. Collegeville, MN: Liturgical. 2003.

Center for the Study of Global Christianity. *Global Christianity*. Gordon Conwell Theological Seminary. (December 2011).

Church of God. http://www.churchofgod.org (accessed September 17, 2017).

Clay, J. Eugene. "The Woman Clothed in the Sun: Pacifism and Apocalyptic Discourse among Russian Spiritual Christian Molokan Jumpers" *Church History 80*, no. 1 (March, 2011): 109-138.

Clement of Rome. "The Epistle of St. Clement of Rome and St. Ignatius of Antioch" in *Ancient Christian Writers*, Trans. James A. Kleist. Westminster, MD: The Newman Press, 1961.

Coleridge, Henry James. *Life and Letters of Francis Xavier.* Monumenta Xaveriana trans. London: Burns and Oats. 1876.

Conybeare, Fredrick Cornwallis. trans. *The Key of Truth: A Manual of the Paulician Church of Armenia.* Oxford: Clarendon. 1898.

Cutten, George Barton. *Speaking with Tongues: Historically and Psychologically Considered.* New Haven: Yale University Press, 1927.

de Cantanzaro, C. J. trans. *Symeon the New Theologian: The Discourses.* New York: Paulist. 1980.

du Bois, Jacques. "Testimony of Jacque du Boise of Monpiellier, January 3 1707" in *Les Prophètes protestants: Réimpression de l'ouvrage institut Le Théâtre sacré des Cévennes, ou récit des diverses merveilles nouvellement opérées dans cette partie de la province du Languedoc.* A. Bost ed. Paris Se vend chez Delay: Paris. 1847.

Enloe, Rob. "Common Barriers to the Baptism of the Holy Spirit", Presented at the *Assemblies of God World Missions Pre-Field Orientation for New Missionaries.* Springfield, MO: Central Bible College. 2013.

Ensley, Eddie. *Sounds of Wonder: A Popular History of Speaking in Tongues in the Catholic Tradition.* New York: Paulist. 1977.

Everts, J.M. "Aorist (Undefined) Adverbial Participles: Exegetical Insight," in *Basics of Biblical Greek Grammar,* by William Mounce, 3rd ed. Grand Rapids, MI: Zondervan. 2009.

Foot Moore, George. *Judaism in the First Centuries of the Christian Era: The Age of Tannaim,* vol. I. New York: Schocken. 1971.

Foster, Kenelm. ed. & trans. "Bernard Gui" in *The Life of St. Thomas Aquinas.* Baltimore: Helicon. 1959.

Eusebius. *The Nicene and Post-Nicene Fathers: The Church History.* V, 16, 2d Ser., Trans. Aurthur McGriffert. Grand Rapids, MI: Eerdmans. 1961.

———. *Ecclesial History,* 5.16.7-21. Peabody, MA: Hendrickson, 1998.

Ganss, George. ed. *Ignatius of Loyola: Spiritual Exercises and Selected Work.* New York: Paulist. 1991.

General Council of the Assemblies of God. *Combined Minutes of the General Council of the Assemblies of God in the United States of America, Canada and Foreign Lands.* Hot Springs, AR: Assemblies of God. 1914.

———. Statistics of the Assemblies of God (USA) 1975-2015. http://agchurches.org/Sitefiles/Default/RSS/AG.org%20TOP/AG%20Statistical%20Reports/2016%20(2015%20reports)/Adhs%20Ann%202015.pdf (accessed September 17, 2017).

Giles, J.A. trans. *Matthew of Paris' English History from about the Years 1235-1273.* Vol. 1, 2. London: Henry G. Bohm. 1852.

Groce, M. ed. & trans. "Vincent Ferrier (Saint)" in *Dictionnaire de Téologie Ctholoque.* Paris: Librairie Litouzey et Ane. 1950.

Guerra, Elena. *First Letter (April 17th, 1895).* http://www.elenaguerra.org/cgi-sys/suspendedpage.cgi?option=com_content&view=article&id=131:first-letter-april-17th-1895&catid=37:correspondencias&Itemid=56 (accessed September 16, 2017).

Hart, Columba, and Jane Bishop. trans. "Hildegard" in *Scito vias Domini*. New York: Paulist. 1990.

Hicks, Cadmus. "Galerius, Valerius Maximianus". In *Who's Who in Christian History*, ed. J. D. Douglas, and P. W. Comfort. Wheaton, IL: Tyndale House. 1992.

Higley, Sarah. *Hildegard of Bingen's Unknown Language: An Edition, Translation, and Discussion*. New York: Palgrave Macmillan. 2007.

Ignatius. "Polycarp", 2:2, *Ingace d'Antioch: Lettres*, 4th ed. Camelot, Paris: 1969. Ronald Kydd Translation.

International Church of the Foursquare Gospel. http://www.foursquare.org/about/stats (accessed September 19, 2017).

International Pentecostal Holiness Church. http://iphc.org/introduction/ (accessed September 19, 2017).

John Paul II. "Private Audience of Pope John Paul II with the ICCRS Council, Rome, December 11, 1979," in *Then Peter Stood Up. . . Collection of the Popes' Addresses to the Catholic Charismatic Renewal from Its Origin to the Year 2000*. Vatican City: International Catholic Charismatic Renewal Services. 2000.

Kelsey, Morton. *Tongues Speaking: An Experiment in Spiritual Experience*. New York: Doubleday. 1968.

Knox, R. A. *Enthusiasm: A Chapter in the History of Religion*. New York: Oxford University Press. 1950.

Kydd Ronald. *Charismatic Gifts in the Early Church: An Exploration into the Gifts of the Spirit During the First Three Centuries of the Christian Church*. Peabody, MA: Hendrickson, 1984.

Lacy, John. *The Spirit of Prophecy Defended*. Edward Irving, ed. Boston: Brill Academic. 2003.

Latourette, Kenneth. *A History of Christianity Volume I Beginnings to 1500*. New York: Harper & Row Publishers. 1975.

Leo XIII, *Divinum Illud Munus: Encyclical of Pope Leo Xiii on the Holy Spirit*. (May 9, 1897). http://w2.vatican.va/content/leo-xiii/en/encyclicals/documents/hf_l-xiii_enc_09051897_divinum-illud-munus.html (accessed September 16, 2017).

Luther, Martin. "Pentecost Hymn of 1524" in *Luther's Hymns*, James Lambert ed. Philadelphia, PA: Philadelphia. 1917.

———. "Small Catechism, Article 3" in *The Book of Concord*. Theodore Gerhardt Tapper ed. Philadelphia: Muhlenberg Press. 1959.

———. "Sermon, Ascension Day 1523" in *Sermons of Martin Luther*, John Nicholas Lenker ed. Grand Rapids, MI: Baker. 1983.

———. "Lectures on Galatians" in *Luther's Works*, vol. 26. St. Louis, MO: Concordia. 1991.

MacArthur, John. *Charismatic Chaos*. Grand Rapids, MI: Zondervan. 1992.

Macchia, Frank. "Sighs Too Deep for Words: Toward a Theology of Glossolalia," *Journal of Pentecostal Theology* 1, 1992), 47-73.

BIBLIOGRAPHY

Maloney, George. ed. "Pseudo-Macarius" in *Fifty Spiritual Homilies; and, the Great Letter*. New York: Paulist. 1992.

Manning, Henry Edward Cardinal. ed. "Bonaventure" in *The Life of St. Francis of Assisi: Chapter 11 – The Spirit of Prophecy*. Rockford, IL: Tan Books, 1988.

Marius, Richard. *Martin Luther: The Christian between God and Death*. Cambridge, MA: Harvard University Press. 1999.

Marshall, Howard. *Luke: Historian and Theologian*. Grand Rapids, MI: Zondervan, 1970.

Martin, Paul, James Book, and David Duncan, *God and Angels*. Springfield, MO: Global University, 1992.

Menzies William, and Robert Menzies. *Spirit and Power: Foundations of Pentecostal Experience*. Grand Rapids, MI: Zondervan, 2000.

Meyer, Robert. ed. *St. Athanasius: Life of Saint Antony*, Ancient Christian Writers. New York: Newman. 1950.

Müntzer, Thomas. "Letter from Thomas Müntzer to Martin Luther, Allstedt, July 9, 1523" in *The Collected Works of Thomas Müntzer*. Peter Matheson ed. Edinburgh, UK: T&T Clark. 1988.

———. "The Prague Protest" in *Revelation and Revolution: Basic Writings of Thomas Müntzer*. Michael Baylor trans, and ed. Bethlehem, PA: Lehigh University Press. 1993.

Kaiser, Walter. *The Promise-Plan of God: A Biblical Theology of the Old and New Testaments*. Grand Rapids, MI: Zondervan. 2008.

Parham, Sarah. *The Life of Charles F. Parham, Founder of the Apostolic Faith Movement*. Joplin, MO: Joplin Printing. 1944.

Paul VI. *Dogmatic Constitution on the Church: Lumen Gentium*. (Vatican: 1964), 12. http://www.vatican.va/archive/hist_councils/ii_vatican_council/documents/vat-ii_const_19641121_lumen-gentium_en.html (accessed September 16, 2017).

———. "Address of Pope Paul VI to the Catholic Charismatic Renewal on Occasion of the Second International Leaders' Conference, Rome May 19, 1973" in *Then Peter Stood Up. . . Collection of the Popes' Addresses to the Catholic Charismatic Renewal from Its Origin to the Year 2000*. Vatican City: International Catholic Charismatic Renewal Services. 2000.

Payne, J. Barton. *The Theology of the Older Testament*. Grand Rapids, MI: Zondervan, 1962.

Pew Research Center. *Global Christianity: A Report on the Size and Distribution of the World's Christian Population*. Washington D.C.: Pew Forum on Religion & Public Life, December 2011. http://www.pewforum.org/files/2011/12/Christianity-fullreport-web.pdf (accessed September 19, 2017).

———. *The Changing Global Religious Landscape*. http://www.pewforum.org/2017/04/05/the-changing-global-religious-landscape/ (accessed October 28, 2017).

Ramabai, Pandita. "A Testimony of Our Inexhaustible Treasure" in *Pandita Ramabai in Her Own Words: Selected Works*. Meera Kosambi ed. New Delhi: Oxford University Press. 2000.

Ranzano, Peter. "Life of St. Vincent Ferrier" in *A Dictionary of Miracles*. E. Cobham Brewer ed. Philadelphia: Lippincott. 1834.

Root, Jean Christie. *Edward Irving: Man, Preacher, Prophet*. Eugene, OR: Wipf & Stock. 2012.

Rudametkin, Maxin. *Selections from the Book of Sprit and Life, Including the Book of Prayers and Songs*. Whittier, CA: Stockton Trade Press. 1966.

Schaff, Phillip. ed. *The Creeds of Christendom, with a History and Critical Notes*, vol. 1, 6th ed. New York: Harper & Brothers. 1877.

———. ed. "Dialogue of Justin, Philosopher and Martyr, with Trypho, a Jew" in *The Ante-Nicene Fathers: The Writings of the Fathers Down to A.D. 325. I*. London: Catholic Way Publishing. 2014. Kindle Edition.

———. ed. "The Didache: The Lord's Teaching Through the Twelve Apostles" in *The Ante-Nicene Fathers: The Writings of the Fathers Down to A.D. 325. I*. London: Catholic Way Publishing. 2014. Kindle Edition.

———. ed. "Against Praxeas" in *The Ante-Nicene Fathers: The Writings of the Fathers Down to A.D. 325. III*. London: Catholic Way Publishing. 2014. Kindle Edition.

———. ed. "Origen Against Celsus" in *The Ante-Nicene Fathers: The Writings of the Fathers Down to A.D. 325. IV*. London: Catholic Way Publishing. 2014. Kindle Edition.

———. ed. "A Treatise of Novation Concerning the Trinity" in *The Ante-Nicene Fathers: The Writings of the Fathers Down to A.D. 325. V*. London: Catholic Way Publishing. 2014. Kindle Edition.

———. ed. "Ten Homilies on the First Epistle of John to the Parthians" in *Nicene and Post-Nicene Fathers. 3*. H. Browne trans. London: Catholic Way Publishing. 2014. Kindle Edition.

———. ed. "The Church History of Eusebius" in *Nicene and Post-Nicene Fathers. 2*. London: Catholic Way Publishing. 2014. Kindle Edition.

Schöler, L. W. *A Chapter of Church History from South Germany*. W. Wallis. trans. London: Longmans, Green, & Co. 1894.

Seymour, William. *Letter to One Seeking the Holy Ghost*. Los Angeles: Apostolic Faith. 1907.

Shaw, P. E. *The Catholic Apostolic Church Sometimes Called Irvingites*. New York: King's Crown Press. 1946.

Stronstad, Roger. *The Charismatic Theology of St. Luke*. Peabody, MA: Hendrickson, 1984.

———. *Spirit, Scripture & Theology: A Pentecostal Perspective*. Baguio City, Philippines: Asia Pacific Theological Seminary Press. 2005.

———. *The Prophethood of All Believers: A Study in Luke's Charismatic Theology*. Cleveland, TN: Centre for Pentecostal Theology, 2010.

Tarr, Del. *The Foolishness of God: A Linguist Looks at the Mystery of Tongues*. Springfield, MO: Access Group, 2012.

Villar, Louis, Marcel Pin, and Jean Cavalier. *Annales du Midi: revue archéologique, historique et philologique de la France méridionale*, Tome 49, no. 193. Nîmes, France: Chastanier frères et Almeras. 1937.

Welch, John. "A Missionary Movement" *Pentecostal Evangel*, no. 366-367. (November 13, 1920): 8.

Wensinck, A. J. trans. "Isaac" in *Mystical Treatises*. Amsterdam: Koninklijke Akademie van Wetenschappen. 1923.

Wesley, John. "Sermon, 'The More Excellent Way'" in *The Works of John Wesley*. Grand Rapids, MI: Baker, 2007.

———. "A Letter to the Reverend Dr. Conyers Middleton" in *The Works of John Wesley*. Grand Rapids, MI: Baker, 2007.

———. "Journal, August 15, 1750" in *The Works of John Wesley*. Grand Rapids, MI: Baker, 2007.

Whittaker, Molly ed. "Hermas" in *Die Apostolischen* Väter I der Hirt des Hermas. Berlin, Germany: Akademie. 1956.

Williams, George. *The Radical Reformation*. Philadelphia: The Westminster Press. 1952.

Youngs, Benjamin. *Testimony of Christ's Second Appearing, Exemplified by the Principles and Practice of the True Church of Christ*. 4th ed. Albany, NY: Van Benthuysen. 1856.

Zander, Valentine. *St. Seraphim of Sarov*. Crestwood, NY: Vladimir's Seminary Press. 1975.